Miriam's World —and Mine

By Rosemary Mild

Author of the 1999 *Miriam's Gift*, a mother's remembrance of her daughter lost on Pan Am 103.

- **Miriam's Gift:** A Mother's Blessings—Then and Now
- **Miriam, Continued:** Love, Lessons and Politics
- **Her Stories, Essays, Poems**

Magic Island Literary Works • Severna Park, MD • 2012

i

Cover design by Mac-in-Town; also by Myrna Mild Spurrier, Jackie Mild Lau and Leah Lau. Interior book design by Larry Mild.

Library of Congress Cataloging-in-Publication Data
Mild, Rosemary P.
Miriam's World—and Mine
Mild, Rosemary P.
ISBN 978-0-9838597-0-3

"Tulips on Trial" appeared in *New Lines from the Old Line State*, An Anthology of Maryland Writers, a Maryland Writers' Association Book, edited by Allyson E. Peltier, 2008; and in *Scribble*, vol. 6, issue 1, 2006.

"Comfort in Cloth: The Syracuse University Remembrance Quilt" first appeared in *Voices*, membership magazine of the New York Folklore Society, Vol. 34, Fall/Winter 2008. Reprinted (slightly excerpted) by permission.

Permission to reprint photographs of the Syracuse University Remembrance Quilt has been given to Rosemary Mild by Syracuse University.

Chapter 10, "Thanks for Everything" by Jake Stigers, was originally published in *Miriam's Gift*. It is included here with additional comments and Miriam's poem. Reprinted with Jake's permission.

Remarks by Michael Chertoff, first Secretary of the Department of Homeland Security, appeared in *Truth Quest*, July 2007, newsletter of the Victims of Pan Am Flight 103.

In Chapter 15 ("270 Betrayals") the quotes by Frank Duggan, president of the Victims of Pan Am Flight 103 Inc., are reprinted by permission.

The quote by Kate White in Chapter 13 ("This Day Is Mine") and on the back cover is reprinted with her permission.

In "A Photo Album" a photo and article published in *The Capital* in 1985 and 1986, respectively, are reprinted by permission of the Capital-Gazette Newspapers.

"Outstanding in the Field" was first published in CRICKET magazine, June 1994, Vol. 21, No. 10 issue. Text © by Rosemary Mild.

The essay "There Are No Small Parts" first appeared in *Dramatics Magazine*, April 1992.

The essay "If Hogarth Had Been a Playwright" first appeared in *Art Times: A Cultural and Creative Journal*, October 1992.

"How to Apply to College: A Sister's Advice" first appeared in the *Washington Post*, December 4, 1992 as "A Sister's Counsel"; and in the *New York Daily News*, April 29, 1997 as "A sister's advice to her college-bound brother."

First Edition 2012

For our beloved grandchildren—
Alena, Craig, Ben, Leah and Emily

For all the winners of Miriam Luby Wolfe
scholarships and awards

For Larry—my husband, my partner, my soul mate

Acknowledgments

I could fill an entire volume with the names of all the family members, dear friends and acquaintances who are fans of *Miriam's Gift*, and continue to grace me with understanding words, thoughts and hugs. You are precious to me. So I shower you all with oceans and galaxies of appreciation for your warmth, love and support. You give me great strength.

I especially thank John and Ann Pollack, my brother and sister-in-law, for their wise critiquing of the earliest version of *Miriam's Gift* and now their critiques of my personal essays; my cousin Sue Baumblatt, who sent "care" packages to Miriam in college and is now a happy reader of Larry's and my novels; and my sister-in-law Mitzie Mild, who cheers me on no matter what my project.

My grateful thanks also to:

The hard-working staffs who administer the Miriam Luby Wolfe scholarships and awards in Maryland: the English Department at Severna Park High School; Children's Theatre of Annapolis; and Temple Beth Shalom in Arnold.

Judith O'Rourke, Director of Undergraduate Studies at Syracuse University. She is always responsive, always there for the families of Pan Am 103.

All the experts from whom I have gleaned information, including Frank Duggan, Brian Murtagh and Richard A. Marquise. Any factual errors are strictly my own.

Harriet Lyons, for her sensitive editing of this book.

Miriam's friends from grade school on. Their loyalty and reminiscences touch my heart.

Contents

FOREWORD

A Major Headache

I HAD A NAGGING HEADACHE, a pounding problem that just wouldn't go away. *Miriam's Gift: A Mother's Blessings—Then and Now* had gone out of print and the supply on my own shelf had seriously dwindled. Each year I present five or six autographed copies to the winners of the scholarships in Miriam's memory. So what options did I have? Consign the book to used copies on Amazon? Just reprint it as is? That wouldn't work. The book ended before the bombers of Pan Am Flight 103 had been apprehended—the bombers of the plane on which my daughter perished on December 21, 1988. How could I ignore all that has happened in the ensuing years? Only one option appealed to me: to write a second edition.

I asked various friends what they thought. One bluntly advised, "Forget it. Let it go." Others were either enthusiastic or tactfully lukewarm. But readers of the first edition told me it's so inspiring that it's the gift that keeps on giving. I have decided to reprise a (very slightly) abridged first edition and share the traumatic, horrendous, heart-warming and uplifting events since 2000. That was the year two Libyan intelligence agents went on trial for the bombing of Flight 103.

Welcome back to Miriam's world—and mine.

Rosemary Mild, 2012

PRAISE FOR *Miriam's Gift*

Miriam's Gift
A Mother's Blessings—Then and Now
by Rosemary Mild

"Mild shares with readers the horrific night she and her husband spent waiting for word from Pan Am. She also describes her own jagged journey from anguish to healing."

—*Syracuse Herald American*

"Mild refuses to let the terrorists who stole her daughter's life defeat her by dragging her down in hatred, preferring to take heart from, and share with the world, *Miriam's Gift—the gift of love.*"

—*Washington Woman*

"Mild's daughter continues to be a beacon of hope and strength to many—even in death." **—*Midweek,*** Honolulu, Hawaii

"A unique account of the Lockerbie outrage from the point of view of a victim's mother." **—*Annandale Observer***, Lockerbie, Scotland

"The book is more than an expression of a mother's grief. It is an expression of the unbounded optimism of a young girl ready to step onto the world's stage. It is Miriam's gift to the reader."

—*Baltimore Sun*

"We come to know Miriam as the people who loved her did, and we ourselves are just as torn by the terrorists' bomb as she was. She becomes our own child, our sister, our friend."

—*Chesapeake Life*

"Your book will be an inspiration to so many others."

—Fox 45, WBFF-TV Baltimore

Miriam's Gift:
A Mother's Blessings—
Then and Now

INTRODUCTION

Miriam, Her Legacy, Her Gift

ON THE DAY SHE WAS MURDERED, on the day she fell 31,000 feet to her death, my only child left us all a profound legacy. I call it Miriam's gift. Miriam herself would have modestly dubbed it friendship, because it came so naturally from her. But the gift extended far beyond the expectations of any camaraderie I have ever known. I hesitate to call it a "power," because that might sound as if it were forced or imposing, which it never was. Perhaps it's a God-given talent—to animate others' lives with brightness despite despair, with freshness in lieu of fatigue, with renewed purpose to replace floundering or misdirection. She asked only to be loved in return.

She had an uncanny intuition and knew instinctively when to intervene in the lives of those close to her, without preaching, without putting you on the defensive. Her insight earned trust and love. There's no telling how many lives were saved, careers launched, feelings mended and angers quelled by her interventions. She was no saint, by any means, but her presence emanated endless energy, capturing and holding your attention for periods longer than you thought possible. You did not select her for a friend. She selected you, and having done so, she forged a stronger-than-steel bond between you. Her list of "friends and relatives to keep in touch with at college" contained fifty-two names. But even this list turned out to be partial, as I discovered from letters written to us from across the nation and, indeed, from across the seas.

In many ways Miriam was larger than life—her vision so vast, her passion to make the world a better place so fervent that her ideals and her joyousness live in all of us who knew her. Her impact on the world was so remarkable for someone only twenty years old that I am still learning new and amazing things about her—and from her.

Miriam didn't walk, she bounced, her luxuriant brown curls bobbing, intense blue eyes sparkling. She embraced life with all the naiveté and enthusiasm of a child discovering her first Lego set—

and with the wisdom to savor every precious moment. She was studying musical theater in London. Five weeks before she died, she wrote in her journal: "The past two days, I've really felt like part of the city—with the pulse of it, the current, its heart. Maybe it's the people I'm getting to know. I'm getting stronger in myself every day."

Until December 21, 1988, I never really thought about acts of terrorism—about the evil terrorists wreak—in any personal way. The murder of Israeli Olympic athletes in Munich, the storming of the Rome airport were abstract news headlines that I read with detached sympathy. But now terrorism has become my own personal tragedy. You see, Miriam was not just my only child. She was my dearest friend, my loving confidante, and truly the center of my universe. When she was deprived of her beautiful young life, I was deprived of my most cherished dreams: dreams of my only child as a college graduate, as a mother, as the culmination of all the talent and intellect and achievement she was so passionately yet methodically building toward.

When my daughter, Miriam Luby Wolfe, was sixteen, she gave me a diary for my birthday, inscribed: "Dear Mom, may all your beautiful memories be recorded here and may we create infinite others in the years to come."

Memories of Miriam are all I can cling to now. The plane bringing her home from London, Pan Am Flight 103, exploded over Lockerbie, Scotland, destroyed by a terrorist bomb. Miriam was twenty years old, one of thirty-five Syracuse University students returning from a semester of study abroad. All 259 passengers and crew members died, along with eleven Lockerbie residents on the ground.

How do you cope when your only child has been murdered? Where do you find the impetus to get up in the morning when the most precious person in your life has been taken away from you? Miriam gave the gift of friendship to others. She gave the gift of herself to me. And this is the journey on which I embark each day—to make my life meaningful without her, to make each day count the way she would expect me to. And because it's what I expect of myself.

Miriam was a singer, an actress, a dancer, a director, a scholar and a prolific writer. Her animated spirit lives on in me every day. I speak of her often—how it was and how it could have been. I do not live in the wake of that terrible day and the terrible way she died—even though I will always remember that it did not have to be that way.

My mission is to keep Miriam and her bountiful spirit alive for generations to come—and to share her with the world. Perhaps through my daughter you will discover your own child's gifts. Your child doesn't have to be an academic superstar or an athlete or talented in the arts to bring you joy. The gift can be a smile, a hug, a kiss. It can be setting the table or offering to wash your car. If your twelve-year-old son comes home with a C in science on his report card instead of the D he got last term, that's a gift. Mostly, it's a gift to himself, but it's also a gift to you, because he responded to your encouragement and confidence in him that he could do better. Maybe your "encouragement" meant some heavy-duty nagging or taking away his TV, cell phone and computer privileges, but it doesn't matter. You worried about him, cared about him and his future—and he knew it.

Appreciate and accept your child's gifts today. Please don't wait till tomorrow.

CHAPTER 1

"I Am a Lover of Life"

SEPTEMBER 1988. LONG BEFORE THE FIRST red and gold leaves fell from our maple trees, I could sense my usual maternal anxiety dropping away. In fact, I felt that I had almost finished my work as Miriam's mother. Not that we wouldn't always remain close and important to one another. Of course we would. But now she had the tools—intellectual, emotional and spiritual—to forge a superb, productive life for herself. I felt this confidence because she was on her way to London in such a pitch of exhilaration. She'd been away from me the whole summer. Her first performing job—singing and dancing in upstate New York, in a tiny rural town, at a huge theme park. And she did it successfully.

Her talent and potential were crystallizing. She didn't just embrace life, she swallowed it whole. When we were together I found myself in the presence of an intellect both penetrating and passionate. She was taking on the world of words and thoughts and reflections with an insatiable appetite. She dove into the arts, sciences and history and strove to master the written and spoken word. In only two years in college, she'd grown from a high school honors English student to a poet, a writer of essays, short stories and poems; an actress, a singer, a dancer, a director and even a budding artist.

After Moses led the Israelites across the Red Sea, his sister, Miriam, led the women in a triumphal song and dance. The name

1

Miriam comes possibly from the Egyptian Meri, which means love. Luby was my mother's name, from Luba, "beloved" in Russian. It was so appropriate to name her after my mother, who was a flamboyant, brilliant and creative woman.

Nobody can describe Miriam better than she can. She told about herself in her application to the Syracuse University International Programs Abroad.

"I Am a Lover of Life"

I am an only child, and because my parents separated when I was nine years old and divorced when I was ten, I am a product of what is commonly called a "broken home." People often expound on the traumatic nature of divorce, focusing particularly on its negative effect on the couple's children. This always gives me pause, because in my case, it was my parents' marriage that proved traumatic. However, my parents' incompatibility as husband and wife in no way prevented them from being wonderful parents to me. On the contrary, they actually complemented each other surprisingly well as parents.

Both Mom and Dad write and edit for a living and are extraordinarily bright, creative and warm people. My love for them is so great that it would be impossible for me to adequately express it in words. So, I've decided to focus on what is probably the greatest gift they've given me and a gift Mom and Dad share: a great love of learning. By this, I do not mean to focus on my parents' prowess in an academic setting. Rather, I'd like to stress that they nurtured me in a way which gave me a burning desire to learn, to take advantage of every opportunity and to appreciate the beautiful things in our everyday life.

My dad is a compulsive reader—I have never been assigned to read any work of fiction, classical or contemporary, that my father did not own or had not read. So, he was a little worried that I was already seven years old and was not an avid reader. I loved to be read to at the time, but rarely did I pick up a book and read to myself.

My dad devised a plan of action. Unbeknownst to me, he ordered a year-long subscription to the Read About Me Book Club. Read About Me books arrived monthly and contained stories of various adventures of ME, MIRIAM WOLFE, three of my friends and my dog!! I was beside myself. I couldn't for the life of me figure out how "they" (the authors) knew all about me. I kept asking Dad the reason, but he wouldn't give up his secret. His only explanation was that the books were magical. And soon, all books held a magic for me. By the time I was eight, I could polish off books with little effort and great joy.

"Books can become some of your best friends, Miriam," my dad would say. "They will never abandon you and will always bring you joy." To this day, nothing has proven him wrong.

Unlike my father, who is very spontaneous and unfocused, my mom is extremely pragmatic and thorough. She taught me the importance of following things through and that if you really want to know something, you should take the initiative to learn it. Mom and I used to watch the news together every evening, or read either the newspaper or *Time* magazine—something relating to current events. Often, I would ask Mom a question about something that confused me. If she couldn't answer immediately, I would forget about the issue—but not for long. The next morning, I would come into the kitchen for breakfast. At my place setting, I would find several reference books with little markers in them. Mom would say, "Remember last night when you asked me . . .? Well, I looked it up and this is what I found." Mom found a way to lovingly teach me the importance of taking advantage of resources available to me.

As I write this, I am struck by the magnitude of this opportunity to go abroad; to be an active part of a theater community so rich in tradition.

My upbringing was somewhat unconventional in that I never really had a childhood! My parents never treated me as if I were a child; they spoke to me as if I were no different from any of their adult friends. As a result, I matured quickly, enjoying the company of my parents and their friends as much as I enjoyed kids my own age. This has proven useful in countless ways. I was exposed to more than other children and I tend to believe that self-expression through the arts was second nature to me because my parents exposed me to such a wide variety of types of music, art and books.

My parents also provided me with unwavering support. They never tried to dissuade me from pursuing a career in the theater. Instead, they taught me the importance of becoming well-rounded and not limiting myself. At first I was angry when they insisted that I not attend a performing arts high school. Then, I discovered how much more I could learn at the wonderful public high school nearby. My senior year was spent studying all the things I had always been interested in: constitutional law, psychology, sociology, Latin, French and an Honors English class. This terrific year illuminated for me one of the main reasons I love theater so much: the theater allows me to explore hundreds of professions and people, with every character I portray. I am a lover of life and I try to fulfill that love by illuminating something about humanity through my art. Many students my age feel a need to numb themselves to the pain they experience by drinking heavily or using drugs. I avoid these things. But, my refusal to "escape" in this way is also related to my fascination with the human condition. I know that pain is necessary for growth and my desires to grow and learn and change are too great for me to jeopardize.

IT DIDN'T take a formal essay assignment for Miriam to reflect on life. She explored feelings and ideas as vigorously as Lewis and Clark explored the West. In her freshman SU journal, she said:

> I wonder what kind of mother I'll be? Do I want to be one at all? So many of my friends here have lousy relationships with their parents. I see some moms using their children as an extension of their designer outfits. The kids decorate their mothers like in the English court paintings of the little boys in their velvet suits and lace collars. And I don't want to be an authoritarian figure, manipulating my kids and molding them into what I think they should be. Nor do I want to be one of them—another sibling, a peer. I'd much rather they consider me a loving mentor who gently shows them the way.

AT TIMES she turned parental. On my fiftieth birthday, when I complained about feeling old, she scolded me: "Mom, you should be ashamed of yourself. You should be glad you're alive and well to enjoy it." I took her words to heart—her best friend's mother was dying of cancer.

A Syracuse drama professor described her as "an extremely inventive and spontaneous young actress." Not surprising—her all-time idol was Carol Burnett. We'd be in a fitting room at Hecht's and, with no introduction, she'd break out into an "Ed, Eunice and Momma" skit, playing all the dysfunctional family parts perfectly. It was so manic and crazy, but I couldn't stop laughing.

Miriam's own talent for seeing deeply into others was not a conscious effort; it came naturally and intellectually, borne of her own insecurities. She too needed to be liked and loved. This insight served her well in her pursuit of the theater. She was a keen student of the characters she played and had more than a passing interest in psychology. There was a thoroughness about the way she approached everything. And she scooped up fresh concepts the way our dog inhaled Alpo.

She had discovered a quote by comedian Stephen Wright. "You'll love it too, Mom. He said: 'The first time I read the dictionary I thought it was a poem about everything.'"

Exactly how I feel. *Merriam-Webster's Collegiate Dictionary* is my favorite book of all time. I have two copies of the eleventh edition: one at my desk and the other in the living room, just a few steps from the kitchen. It's my adviser and friend.

Miriam was determined to get a well-rounded liberal arts education—despite the possessive schedule of the drama department. "I signed up for a history course on the world wars," she reported on the phone. But a week later, I heard a different story. "Mom, I got to class the first day and—guess what? It's a course for ROTC students. The textbook for World War I alone is 700 pages. You wouldn't believe the detail—panzer division movements, inch by inch. My luck," she sighed. "I guess I'll stick it out, though." She did, and escaped the carnage with a C.

But it was the arts that stoked her fires. "Berthold Brecht really inspires me," she wrote in her journal:

> Brecht is committed to art which serves a purpose other than to amuse. In *Three Penny Opera* he creates theater which would initiate change. I think the power of his plays comes largely from his 'black humor,' which cajoles the audience into laughing and then shames them for doing so. His techniques are amazing. His characters stop in the middle of scenes, walk out on long runways and lecture the audience. And he gets away with it! The result is that he enlightens and educates people so that they, in turn, can act out against social injustices. I think Brecht is as much a social worker as he is a playwright. That's one of my goals—to write plays with his kind of power. I want to move audiences, to stir them into action.

SEPTEMBER 1988. Miriam's father and I had been divorced

for nine years. Our mutual anger long over, we were, at last, two contented families—which gave our daughter a well-deserved measure of peace. When she was eleven, Jim remarried—another woman named Rosemary, believe it or not, and Miriam inherited a stepbrother, Chris Spencer. She was thrilled to no longer be an only child. "I have a brother now!" she told her best friend.

Now that she was on her way to London, I was actually beginning to relax for once in my life, not only as a mother, but as a new wife. Larry and I had been married ten months, and at age fifty-three I still walked around like a newlywed. He was so kind and caring that I felt like a cherished bride. (And I still do after twenty-three years!) I had also settled comfortably into my new job as an engineering writer for Westinghouse. Larry was an electrical engineer at Honeywell and being in such closely allied industries gave us even more in common.

I discovered too that I had inherited an exceptional new family. Often when individuals remarry in midlife they bring emotional baggage and like-them-or-not extra family to the marriage. But not in my case. I discovered, instead, how gentle and affectionate my new stepdaughters and their husbands were. Miriam now had two super-smart stepsisters who were both artists. After our wedding, Jackie said, "It's going to be fun having a baby sister." In the coming weeks, we were to be blessed with our first grandchildren.

Here are Larry's recollections on his encounters with his future stepdaughter:

The night I met Miriam for the first time, she virtually filled the room with her presence. She was so natural and so wonderfully explosive. It was the highest level of exuberance born of a need to share her life's experiences and discoveries. I had never met anyone quite like her. This animated enthusiasm extended to every surface and limb of her long, lean, ever-dancing frame. Her shoulders, arms and hands covered almost as much space as her feet as she gracefully darted about. I found it hard work for my eyes to follow her. Her warm and laughing smile drew you to listen and you dared not let go for fear that you would miss some of the charming and interesting things she had to say. My being there, a total stranger, had not inhibited her in the least.

Larry is such an attentive, diplomatic listener. The truth is she talked his ear off for four hours, even in the car, barely pausing to give the waiter her order at the Wooden Nickel.

During those first days of their getting acquainted, I saw my daughter through Larry's eyes. Weren't everybody's kids this intense? I guess not. Sometimes her sensitivity to others' needs almost overwhelmed her. When she hung up the phone after an hour of listening to a college friend in crisis, she herself was in tears. "I wish there was something I could do for her. I know—I'll send her Shel Silverstein's *Where the Sidewalk Ends*. That'll cheer her up." Then there was the telephone with our twenty-five-foot cord. She'd pace from kitchen to dining room, back through the kitchen and into the living room. If we'd had cell phones then, she'd have walked miles during each conversation. But she also stopped long enough to doodle on any piece of paper on the kitchen table. I'd come down to breakfast wondering, Now where is my grocery list? It was still there, but unrecognizable, hidden among exotic critters and squiggles.

I spent so much time doing the formal parenting thing ("Got your book bag?" "Wear a jacket, it's cold out") that I didn't spend enough time just talking with Miriam. I'm hooked on the TV show *Brothers and Sisters*. What astounds me is the sizzling, often combative conversations, the arguments, the talked-out misunderstandings. Never in my entire growing up did we have such sessions in my house, where my parents' authority ruled.

When Larry came on the scene, he stepped into the role of friendly debater—not planning to; it came naturally to him. We were on our way to a holiday party, sponsored by the Society of Professional Journalists, at the H.L. Mencken House in Balti-more. In the car, a heated exchange nearly boiled over. I had had a nasty car accident and was cited for reckless driving. Lucky for me, the case was dismissed; the other driver and arresting officer didn't show up in court.

Miriam retorted, "Mom, you didn't deserve to get off like that. You were guilty, you should've been punished."

"You know, Miriam," Larry interjected, "your mother actually did get punished. She got three points on her license and eleven stitches in her head."

She frowned, unconvinced that justice had been served. With her college freshman fervor and idealism, she seemed to set even tougher standards for me than she did for the rest of the world.

A year later, on our first anniversary, she sent us one of our most treasured possessions, a card adorned with a teddy bear.

Dear Mom and Larry—It is unbearable to be here in London when what I want to do is to wish you a beary, beary HAPPY ANNIVERSARY! I couldn't be happier for you. You both have taught me a great deal about love and you have an equal partnership that most marriages never achieve. The success of your marriage is not due to luck or chance: you both are extraordinarily giving individu-als, which helps you to compromise when necessary. The harmony you have achieved in your relationship spills over into my life and I'm very grateful for that. You are both such special people. You deserve the best that life has to offer. And you have found it—in each other. May your relationship continue to blossom and change and grow forever. All my love, Miriam.

TO SEND us this card, she had to reach the point where she no longer agonized over the prospect of feeling abandoned, of losing her mother. Did she reach this point easily? Absolutely not.

CHAPTER 2

Bridges to London

"MORNING, ROSEMARY, HEY, you look beat."

"It's that obvious?" I asked, slumping into my chair.

My co-worker Dianne nodded sympathetically.

"Yeah, I'm totally worn out from packing Miriam up for England."

"She's not going back to Syracuse?"

"Not till January. She's spending the first semester of her junior year in London. It's a fabulous place for a musical theater major."

What I didn't reveal was our sour goodbye. It was already three o'clock when I dropped her off at BWI. I had to get to work, but wanted to make sure she was okay. I hastily parked at the No Standing curb and rushed inside, breathless, to the ticket counter. Standing in line, she greeted me in a voice the entire airport could hear: "Mom, take a pill." Jeez, so much for sentimental partings. Early next morning, my phone rang.

"Hi, Mom!"

"Miriam! What's wrong? Are you okay? Where are you?"

"I'm in London, of course. Nothing's wrong, Mom, I'm fine."

"You sound like you're around the corner. Why are you calling?"

"I miss you, Mom."

"I miss you too, dear, but . . ." I waited for the other shoe to drop. "How was the flight?"

"Fine. The whole London-Syracuse gang was aboard and I made lots of new friends. We talked our way across the Atlantic. Mom, we found this great flat in Elgin Crescent. It's only a few minutes' walk to my classes. It was a little more expensive than some, but we wanted to be in a safe neighborhood."

"It sounds like you made a good choice. When do your classes start?"

"Tomorrow."

"This is getting to be an expensive call, darling, and it's only your first day there."

"Don't be angry, Mom."

"I'm not." (Angry, no. Ticked off, yes.)

"Bye. I love you."

"I love you too, dear."

I flopped into bed that night feeling reassured. She'd arrived safely, she chosen a good flat. And she missed me. This thought buoyed me up and suppressed the undertow of my other thought—that this was going to be an expensive four months.

The next morning, I barely stepped through my office door when I hear my phone ring with ominous urgency. I dumped my briefcase and purse on my desk and grabbed for the handset, nearly dropping it on the floor.

At first I hear nothing and then—

"Mom!"

Her voice came through louder than usual and rife with anxiety. She hadn't even been gone forty-eight hours. "Miriam, what's wrong? We spoke yesterday."

"Mom! This is an extreme emergency. I did something stupid."

"What? Tell me already." My heart beat faster.

"I was robbed. They took my new wallet."

"You mean you were held up at gunpoint?"

"No! I mean someone swiped the wallet from my purse. I

had it hanging on the back of my chair."

"Where were you? Didn't you or anyone see it?"

"No, Mom, no one. We were sitting in a restaurant eating and minding our own conversations. We had just settled on the flat and stopped off for a bite to eat. It was like a little celebration."

"You still have your purse with the Traveler's Cheques in it—don't you?" Silence. "Don't you?"

"No, they fit so nicely in the new wallet Larry gave me . . ." Her voice trembled.

Larry had taken a business trip to London in July and surprised her with a Velcro wallet, sized to accommodate the larger British bills. In it he'd tucked $175 in British currency. The Travelers Cheques I had purchased were for room, board and incidentals.

"Have you been to American Express yet?" I asked.

"Yes, that's where I'm calling from, but I need the serial numbers for the Travelers Cheques."

"Don't tell me they were in the wallet, too?"

"Uh-huh. Don't be angry, Mom. I made another copy of the list at home, just like you told me to. I thought I brought it with me, but I can't find it. I think I left it in the desk in my room, top center drawer. I need for you to get it and read the numbers over the phone to me."

"You realize, of course, that I'm at work."

"Sure, Mom, I'm calling you there, aren't I? But I do need for you to go home and get the list now and call me back. I'll wait here for you. I don't have any money."

I swiveled my chair around, pondering what to do next. Dianne was tactfully trying to pretend she hadn't heard a word. Miriam's bossy side even on the phone always raised the decibels to an embarrassing degree. I wondered how many of my other co-workers were also listening.

"Okay," I reluctantly agreed. Never mind that I was trying to meet a deadline. I took down the American Express phone number in London and left for home. The list was exactly where she said it was and I called her back.

"Thanks so much, Mom. You know, I feel really bad. I was planning to go to the bank right from the restaurant to deposit my cash. Larry was so generous to me. I love you. Love to him, too."

After I hung up, I felt guilty (how like me to blame myself). Why didn't I take a few minutes when we were packing to warn her about guarding her purse?

Her first letter to us:

Dear Mom and Larry:

The postal strike ended yesterday. I'm relieved. I really needed to get letters off to friends—and family, of course. Yesterday was also our last day of freedom before classes began. It's days without any structure that really start to wear on my sanity. I wonder why I feel so worthless—a feeling of guilt inside about not having seen/done certain things, yet logic tells me there's plenty of time.

I love our room. It's substantially smaller than Christine and Robin's, but I like it. Our apartment has huge windows and high ceilings—a great place for sleeping during the day like Wyeth's *Daydream* (the Helga pictures). The walls of our flat are a very soothing cream in the living room, which is decorated in pink, light green and gray. My room has really light green walls with a bedspread in purply red and white. Jessica and I have matching bears sitting on our beds.

Christine and Robin know a whole group of great Irishmen and brought them over last night! We had a wonderful time. They are much more gentleman-like than American men!

Today was the first day of classes. My classes are lots o' work! Intense! I love London. I can't wait till I've found favorite places: to spend time, to relax, to study, to dance, to gather my thoughts. I really want to get off the beaten track—meet many Brits, get to know them. Well, I gotta go. I'm off to Harrod's to listen to upper-class British accents. Much love.

ONLY a few days passed before her next call. "Mom, I've landed an internship at the King's Head Theater Club. It's a very innovative and prestigious company. They have a trainee program that has produced careers on Broadway and in London's West End and Royal Shakespeare circles."

"You're already taking twenty-one credits, plus voice lessons," I reminded her. "You told me you and Jessica are taking more credits than any of the others in your group. How in the world will you find time for this? And how about the field trips in Art History and Architecture—won't they conflict?"

"Don't worry, Mom. I'll be working on Fridays—we don't have any classes Fridays. I'll be working the box office and running lines with auditioning actors."

"That's great, dear," I said weakly.

A few weeks and a dozen calls later, my phone rang at work. This time a weepy voice confronted me. "Mom, there's something we have to talk about." I waited in silence. Now what?

"When I called to tell you about the internship you were so cool about it. I expected you to be enthusiastic and I cried hysterically when I got off the phone."

I was glad she couldn't see me smiling over her melodrama. But her next words astonished me.

"Mom, we were both wrong. I was working so hard for them and at first I loved it. But after awhile they seemed to be taking me for granted. I did miss some class trips, too. Anyway, I quit. I wrote them a nice note to thank them for giving me the opportunity." Mini-crisis over.

A postcard to Larry and me . . .

We went to Wilton and saw this magnificent collection—Rembrandt, Rubens, Reynolds, Gainsborough and, of course, Brueghel. (I thought of you, Mom—don't you love Brueghel!?!) We also went to Stourhead Garden in Wiltshire—It's the closest thing to Heaven on Earth. We were all so overwhelmed we couldn't even speak!

IN HER cards and letters she reminded me of the figures in some of Chagall's paintings. They float in air just from the sheer jubilation of being. She wrote to her new sister in Honolulu:

Dear Jackie—CONGRATULATIONS! Alena Grace Lau, a beautiful name for a beautiful child! I just heard the news. Wow! I can't wait to lend a hand in spoiling my new niece rotten! I want so much to call you—but the cost of phoning halfway around the world is really prohibitive.

I'm doing well—classes are INSPIRING! I'm taking, in addition to theater classes, Britain through Architecture and Art History! Jackie, we'll have so much to talk about when I return!! I love and miss you.

MID-NOVEMBER, another call from London: "Mom, I'm sending Grandpa Saul his card for his eighty-third birthday."

"His birthday was October 24th."

"Mom, why didn't you remind me? I can't believe you didn't. I thought his birthday was November 24th. I've had his card for three weeks!"

I was ticked off at her for talking to me that way, but I kept my mouth shut. I was not about to start an argument at work.

The next day she called again. I steeled myself. "Mom," she said, "I apologize for talking to you like that yesterday. It was my responsibility to remember Grandpa's birthday." My mouth dropped open. I felt like saying: Dear, would you please repeat that while I hold the phone up so my whole office can hear?

By the next week she's moved on to politics. It was her first presidential election and I had sent her an absentee ballot. Another

15

phone call. She needed information on the candidates. I expounded for several minutes, quite knowledgeably, I thought, but I was kidding myself.

"No, Mom, I need more than that. What about the congressmen and judges and county council? I'll call you back tomorrow."

"Never mind," I said. "I'll mail you a few pounds of *Washington Post* and *Capital* articles." She cast her vote for Michael Dukakis.

My pleas to curtail her phone calls didn't sink in. She called my father in Milwaukee:

"Grandpa Saul's not home? I'll call him back another time. But how are you, Hilda?" She chatted with his housekeeper for thirty minutes. As the time drew nearer to come home, her calls to friends in the States multiplied like blades of crabgrass on our front lawn. It was her way of reconnecting. The phone bills for her last seven weeks in London: $537.

Miriam showered her letters and cards with exclamation points. For her, life was an exclamation point. With her long, lean frame topped by a burst of curls, you could almost say that she herself was an exclamation point.

In her journal she wrote:

Just got back from Manchester Square where the Wallace Collection is. What an absolutely wonderful museum! Fragonard's *The Swing* is there. I could not stop looking at it—it's exquisite. So whimsical. Rembrandt's *Artist's Son* is so breathtaking that I had to look at it for ten minutes.

Went to Bath yesterday—great city. The bus ride there gave me my first glimpse of some of the most beautiful countryside I've ever seen. The grass was so green that in some areas it looked fluorescent. Beautiful little villages with cows on the hills and sheep. Bath itself has almost entirely Georgian architecture. It has limestone buildings that are straightforward—no ornate crap. The Clean Air Act just went into effect there. All the buildings are being cleaned. The ones not yet cleaned have brown stains covering them and the clean ones are a light honey color. We saw the Roman baths. We'd all like to go back to Bath— four hours just wasn't enough.

THE DAY after the High Holy Days she called to wish Larry and me a Happy New Year. "Guess what, Mom. I attended Yom Kippur services at an Orthodox synagogue, but women aren't allowed to sit downstairs. I protested, but it didn't do any good."

"Of course not," I told her. "That's the Orthodox custom." I sighed. "Couldn't you have saved your feminist crusading for some other time?"

"There's no wrong time, Mom."

We talked about the course she would start teaching January 6 at the Youtheatre Institute in Syracuse—Beginning Acting for seven- to ten-year-olds.

"Have you done any lesson planning?" I asked.

"Mom, I've been lesson planning for a year and a half."

Teaching was one of her great loves, along with writing and the theater. In her journal she listed some ideas for the course and then added: "I just learned something about teaching: Never show openly, in front of a group of students, that you are frustrated by a certain student's lack of understanding. Don't assume the student hasn't been paying attention. Give him the benefit of the doubt."

On a field trip:

Hi, Mom and Larry—I'm lying here, in my hotel room in Amsterdam! This city is beautiful and full of things to do.

We left on Thursday night at 6. We took a nice coach (they hate the word "bus"!) to drive to the ferry. What I thought would be a crude sort of boat turned out to be a cruise ship that would've put the Love Boat to

17

shame! It was sooo huge and we drove our bus right into the hull, where there was a parking lot that housed about twenty-five buses. The ship was three stories high: it had three restaurants, two casinos, two movie theaters, a piano bar and lounge, and a disco!! It was an eight-hour boat ride. Jess and I shared an adorable little cabin.

Our first day in Amsterdam was incredible! We got up early, had breakfast and set out to see the Anne Frank Museum: the actual annex where the Franks were in hiding from July 6, 1942 to August 1, 1944. It has been preserved and it is the most powerful exhibit I've ever experienced. Christine, Jess and I all cried. The panels in the museum include quotes from Anne's diary (which I've read many times). It's so infuriating to think that this gifted, insightful, articulate girl could have made a great contribution to this world had she been allowed to live. And she's one of six million. It was the most emotionally draining museum in the world.

Then, we went to the Stedelijk Museum. We saw incredible work by Kandinsky, Chagall, Jasper Johns, Van Gogh, Cezanne and the most beautiful Matisse cutout in existence. It was breathtaking!

We snapped pictures galore while walking around the city. Holland has the most beautiful people I've ever seen—all the people here are blond. The women wear very little makeup, they are all at least five foot eight, thin and fashionably dressed. The men are tall, blond and blue-eyed with chiseled Scandinavian features. I literally have not seen one unattractive person in Amsterdam!

Being a pedestrian here is a major hazard. Not only must you worry about the insane drivers and the trams, you must avoid the majority of Amsterdam citizens who zoom around on BICYCLES! It's really a charming idea, but downright hazardous in practice. The cyclists are beautiful, cosmopolitan Dutch people who are OUT FOR

BLOOD!! We've had quite a few close calls!

Anyway, that's Amsterdam for you! It's been exhausting, but very educational and fun. Mom, you'd love this city—it's architecturally FASCINATING—no two buildings are alike.

WELL, well, well. Someone was growing up. Architecture has been a fascination of mine since Art 11 at Smith. But one Saturday at the Baltimore Inner Harbor, when I stopped to gaze at details high up on an Art Deco building, she protested. "Mom, you're embarrassing me."

Dear Dad, Rosemary and Chris:

Bonjour! We just got back from a field trip to Paris. We took a bus to Dover (as in the "white cliffs of") and then caught a ferry to Calais, where we spent our first night. The next day, our bus took us straight to Versailles. It was awe-inspiring to be there, but I hate ornateness without purpose in architecture! Versailles is so overly ostentatious; I find it vulgar. But I guess the bourgeoisie felt the same way during the French Revolution. The gardens at Versailles are a sight to behold. They are all organized in unique shapes, as though they're meant to be viewed from the top, like an Esther Williams film! We were lucky—the weather was BEAUTIFUL the entire weekend.

We were finally taken to our hotel. My art history professor decided that it'd be neat for us to stay in the area of the city where artists such as Picasso and Degas lived. So she chose the Hotel Pigalle. Pigalle is the most notoriously seedy part of Paris. Our professor forgot that safety as well as historical trivia is important when choosing a hotel! The rooms themselves were nice, though, thank God. We could see Sacre Coeur in the distance and nothing but strip joints in the immediate area. What a weird dichotomy!

By the time we had cleaned up and eaten dinner, it was 10:30 at night. So Heather, Lisa and I decided we wanted to walk to the Eiffel Tower and L'Arc de Triomphe. Great idea. Little did we know that the half-inch distance on our map meant a walk that would take us till 1 a.m. But, despite our exhaustion, we enjoyed seeing Paris at night on foot. Surprisingly, it's a really safe city. In many ways, it's safer than London. I think I'm the only person to have seen the Eiffel Tower be turned off: they actually un-light it at 1 a.m. We were standing there, triumphant after our walk of miles and suddenly, section by section, someone turned off the tower. It was actually pretty funny. We didn't get home till 3 a.m.

Saturday was the most amazing day of all—we went to the Musée d'Orsay first. It has every painting you've ever dreamed of seeing! Afterwards, we ate at a beautiful outdoor cafe: *le fromage et une baguette.* I spoke French the whole time! It was great fun.

We had to leave for Calais on Sunday afternoon. In the morning we went to the Louvre. I was really disappointed: it was such a mob scene. (Sunday is the only day the Louvre is free, so everyone in Paris was there!) And, despite the guard yelling 'No flash' every three seconds, people insisted on taking flash pictures of the Mona Lisa. I was livid—these people are destroying a magnificent work of art because they have to have a snapshot (which probably won't even come out—the Mona Lisa is behind a glass case)!! The best part about the Louvre was outside: they have trucks that sell CHOCOLATE CREPES that they make in front of you! Just like hot dogs or pretzels in NYC!!

So, all in all, Paris was WONDERFUL. I'm anxious to hear from you (especially my red-headed brother who whet my palate by writing me a letter!). Keep it up, dear brother, 'cause I miss talkin' to you.

MY PSYCHOANALYST father laughed aloud when he read the following note. He got such a kick out of her intellectual exuberance.

> Dear Grandpa Saul—Happy Chanukah! I have only nine more days before we'll be on the same continent again! This unique opportunity to learn here in London has been the most amazing three and-a-half months of my life. I saw a terrific play recently that made me think about you: it's called *Mrs. Klein*, about child psychoanalyst Melanie Klein. I was so fascinated and enthralled by it that I bought a dictionary of psychoanalytic words. We'll have to talk in depth when I return.

A LETTER from one of her dear friends bubbled over with the joy of their London life:

> Dear Rosemary—Miriam and I were flatmates in London. Your daughter was the most blessed person to ever enter my life—that is what I would have you know, again and again.
>
> Did she ever tell you about Matthew? It seemed as though dashing men were forever falling in love with Miriam; while she was working at the theater, she met this gentleman and spent time with him outside work. He was very witty and artistic. She used to go out with him for dinner and when she got home, she'd recline across the end of my bed, head on one hand, eyes twinkling and tell me how delightful he was.
>
> The last Saturday before we left London, a group of us went to Oxford for the day. Mir and I split from the group and strolled around the quaint town, admired the extraordinary school buildings, shopped (of course—we both bought a copy of *Desiderata* and an Oxford sweatshirt). We

took pictures of children who were rehearsing a play in a church and climbed up to the tower to see the city. We leaned on the ancient stones, enjoying a breathtaking view, when I spotted a tower across the city I liked better.

"I wish we were on that balcony, Mir," I told her. She said, "The tower's always greener on the other side of the city, Christine."

The night we all finished our finals, we went to the Hard Rock Cafe. Miriam ordered a Blue Hawaiian. It looked like Windex in a fishbowl and we laughed for ten minutes.

One more thing—Do you remember a picture of yourself sitting on Mir's bed at school? You are holding hands and both laughing joyously. She carried it everywhere and showed it off whenever she explained how wonderful you are. Love, Christine.

I had a flash of jealousy—the secret life of my daughter? She'd never told me about Matthew. Another letter to us:

This semester has been so incredible. I've seen twenty-six plays! My favorites were *Cat on a Hot Tin Roof, Les Miserables, Uncle Vanya, Mrs. Klein, A Moment Too Late* and *Our Country's Good.*

I'm sitting on a bench in a small park near High Holborn Street. Though the sky is completely gray, it's warm and the leaves that are left on the trees are bright yellows, pinks and salmons. The morning has been quite fun. The Covent Garden/Charing Cross area of the city has all the hustle and bustle of every clichéd song in existence: children laughing, people passing, silver bells. Actually, there's a food shop with bells that sound on the hour. I went inside and the whole place smelled of cinnamon and spice. Mom, when I get home, can we have a little party just for our women friends? We'll make tea and scones.

THE PROSPECT warmed my heart. It would be our first party together as adults. Three days before her return from London, she called. "Mom, I'm worried. I only have an hour between planes at JFK. With customs and everything and if the plane is late . . . what if I can't make my connection to BWI?"

I was worried too. "Call you right back," I said.

After making an additional reservation for her on a flight leaving half an hour later, the last one to BWI, we talked again. "If you miss the last flight out," I told her, "stay at an airport hotel. Don't sit in the airport all night. Are you feeling okay?" I asked. "You sound kind of hoarse."

"I am. I think I'm getting the flu."

"Dear, get right into bed and stay there. Drink lots of juice."

"Thank you, Mom, I will." I could hear the relief in her voice. "I love you," she said.

"I love you too, darling." It was our last conversation.

CHAPTER 3

And the Earth Turned Its Face

THE EARTH TURNS ITS FACE THE FARTHEST from the sun today, as if hiding in shame, as it does for the winter solstice every year. Nevertheless, December 21, 1988, moved innocently along, with no foreshadowing of the tragic evil in store for it.

Our last workday before the holidays dawned with gray skies and a raw cold, but Larry and I drove to our respective offices in high spirits. Miriam was coming home at eleven tonight. All our plans were in place for her homecoming. After a few days with us, she would spend a week with her father in Virginia and then a second week with Larry and me in south Florida—days we would jealously guard from time planned with her friends. I couldn't wait to share my favorite places with her: the historic Italian villa Vizcaya; Wolfie's with its succulent half-sours and blueberry cheesecake; tennis at Flamingo Park. Early in January she'd fly to Syracuse to begin her part-time job teaching acting to children. Then the new semester would begin.

I was swept up in the excitement of the holidays. The world was shopping and partying its way through the glitziest month of the year. Miriam was coming home. Such anticipation and promise.

The hours flew. In my office at Westinghouse, the last of the prevailing publications miraculously churned their way glitch-free through the editorial mill. We were packing our personal things and office supplies into cartons to prepare for new furniture that would be in place upon our return. Larry planned to leave his office early for a holiday reception at his boss's home. At three o'clock I labeled my last box and chatted over the top of my cubicle partition. The phone rang.

"Rosemary, it's Myrna." Her voice sounded flat, hushed and without emotion, so untypical of my usually animated younger stepdaughter.

"Hi, Myrna, I don't think you've ever called me at the office before. What a pleasant surprise."

"Rosemary!" This time her voice sounded more ominous. She was calling from their time-share in Ocean City.

"What is it, Myrna?"

"When is Miriam coming home?" she asked.

"Tonight, but you won't be able to see her until tomorrow, she's not coming till eleven."

"What airline is Miriam coming home on?" At first I thought Myrna wanted to meet her flight at BWI.

"Is it Pan Am?" she asked.

"Yes."

"What flight?"

Now I was confused. Why was she asking me this? I knew the flight number by heart, but suddenly I couldn't remember it. "It's Flight 102 or 103, I think, but I'll have to check on the bulletin board at home. Why?"

Myrna's voice dropped to almost a whisper. "There's been an accident."

I didn't ask her any questions. I was too afraid. Afraid to hear the answers. My heart raced. Maybe if I didn't find out any details her words wouldn't be real. I barely said goodbye and started dialing Pan Am. The line was busy. My finger frantically stabbed at the numbers. Busy. Again and again. I dropped the receiver and grabbed my purse. Moments later, I ran down the hall and out the door to my car. I had to get home.

A co-worker called out to me, "Would you like me to drive

you home?"

"No," I said, my voice shaking, "Thanks, anyway. I'm not going to assume the worst." But I did assume the worst. I didn't even turn on the radio as was my custom during the twelve-mile ride home. Was it Miriam's flight or not? I feared that if I heard something horrible on the news I'd lose control of my car. I gripped the steering wheel hard and tried not to think.

I ran into the house and turned on the TV. What confronted me was a grim Dan Rather standing before a room-size photo of the remains of Pan Am Flight 103. The fuselage and cockpit lay on the ground like some great broken dead beast. Sirens and flashing lights pierced the black night.

"The plane exploded at 31,000 feet," I heard Dan Rather say, "over Lockerbie, Scotland." Lockerbie, Scotland? I'd never even heard of the place. I turned off the TV. I was terrified. I was also disoriented and confused. I ran to our bulletin board in the back hall. Maybe, just maybe, 103 wasn't Miriam's flight after all. But it was.

Again and again I tried to reach Pan Am. Nothing but busy signals. My finger ached from dialing our old rotary phone in the kitchen that we'd never gotten around to replacing. In desperation I called the International Programs Abroad office at Syracuse. The woman on the other end, obviously upset and sympathetic, gave me another Pan Am number that she said might be more accessible. It wasn't.

And then I did something thoroughly off the wall: I started dusting. People would be coming, I told myself. Dusting? It was irrational, but I didn't know what else to do. I didn't want to call Larry at his boss's house until I had some concrete facts to tell him. And I still tried not to panic. The kitchen clock showed 5:05. The silence screamed at me. I felt as if I was the only person left in the whole world. I threw the dust cloth back in its drawer and paced the kitchen floor like a caged animal, my breath short. Once more I tried dialing Pan Am. Both numbers buzzed busy, as if to mock me, over and over again. Why wasn't Pan Am calling me, why wasn't somebody helping me?

Finally, I did call Larry, my voice trembling so badly I could hardly ask for him. Laughter and party chatter floated in the background. "Larry has already left," I was told. At 5:30 when my husband stepped through the front door, he found me huddled in a frozen, crouched position on the bottom step of the stairs. My face told him everything.

Increasingly desperate and frantic, I resumed dialing Pan Am. But no matter how often I tried, the line was busy. I had nowhere to turn. Miriam's friends began calling. J.B. in a forced, perky voice, "Hi, Mrs. Mild, is Miriam there?" Perhaps he was pretending he didn't know anything and hoped he was wrong; but I'm pretty sure he already suspected. I answered, "No," and I can't remember what else. I remember everything of that night—and nothing. Many of the details are horribly burned in my brain and others I hardly fathom at all, even after two decades. Our closest friends, four couples, started silently drifting into the house. We hadn't called them. A wave of denial swept over me. What were they doing here, what did they know that I didn't know? But I didn't ask them.

By now it was 9 p.m, the time Flight 103 should have landed at JFK International Airport. Still there was no word from Pan Am.

"You should eat something," somebody said. I felt sick to my stomach and at the same time starved, so I mixed up some instant oatmeal, swallowed one bite and felt like throwing up. I scraped the whole bowlful into the garbage. At the dining room table, several of our friends were gathered in silence. Denial swept over me once more.

"Miriam sent us the most wonderful anniversary card," I announced, smiling as if she was just out for the evening and would walk in the door at any moment. I took it off the buffet and read it aloud.

The hours ticked away relentlessly and we were still in the dark. Had Miriam missed her plane? Not likely. Even though as a teenager she had a habit of "running late" (a perpetual source of annoyance to me, the promptness bug), this was a group flight she was on and the students were going to Heathrow Airport on the bus together. If Miriam had missed her plane or changed her flight, she would have called us. She always called, she never left me hanging. She was just plain considerate.

"Rosemary," Larry called from the kitchen, where he was holding the phone, his hand over the receiver. "It's Rabbi Klensin. He wants to know if we'd like him to come over. He wants to help." Our rabbi had been more than a spiritual leader for me and Miriam. He and his family had been friends as well as neighbors for years. I pushed my fist against my mouth and tried to think what to say.

"Tell him—" I was glad it was Larry who had to deal with it. "Tell him no, but thank you. If he comes it will make it more real." As much as I wanted and needed his comfort, his presence would only confirm my loss. I needed to deny the horror of it even if it was only for a little while longer. Larry thanked him and told him not to come. He understood.

By now we had called the rest of my family. In Milwaukee my father was watching the *MacNeil/Lehrer News Hour* during his dinner, not having the slightest inkling that the news of Pan Am Flight 103 meant his adored first grandchild was probably dead. I heard a long silence before he began choking and sobbing.

At 12:30 a.m. I finally reached Pan Am. I was struck by the cold, businesslike manner of the agent, not even a hint of kindly sympathy in her voice.

"Was my daughter on Flight 103?" I asked weakly.
The icy, dispassionate voice said: "There's an M. Wolfe on the manifest." Still I clung to a naive glimmer of hope. M. Wolfe was a common name. But then the agent told me the final piece of information that crushed any hope: the contact number they had for M. Wolfe was Miriam's phone in her London flat.

I hung up, once more crouched down into a fetal position on the stairs and buried my head in my knees. I couldn't cry. I just doubled up in actual physical pain. "I'd like everybody to leave," I whispered. They were my best friends, but all I could think was, they all have their children.

A surge of disbelief overcame me. This can't have happened, this is preposterous. I had spent my whole life nurturing Miriam, encouraging her to cultivate her talents, teaching her to become a strong, independent and resourceful woman. I had spent my whole life protecting her, for God's sake. When she was small, I had never let her play outside alone after dark. That summer when I was too busy at work to drive her to get her passport, I sent her to Washington on the Metro. That night at dinner she said, "It was a bad neighborhood, Mom." And I felt guilty.

The waiting was over, but the nightmare has just begun, blasting me into the endless black tunnel that would be the rest of my life. Never again would I be able to put my arms around my daughter. Never again would she lay her head on my shoulder.

At 1 a.m. a deadly silence enshrouded the house and I didn't dare think. But I didn't consciously shut down. My brain took pity on me and shielded me from asking unbearable, unanswerable questions: Where is Miriam now? Is she lying on the bitter cold ground in the snow or in cruel pounding rain and mud with nobody there to tenderly cradle her broken body? I wanted to scream: "Did she suffer? Somebody please tell me No!"

As Larry and I dragged ourselves upstairs, I mentally sealed myself off from the futility of these images. I squashed them like I squashed the ugly, jumping crickets that invaded our basement every fall. Heading straight for Miriam's room, I gritted my teeth and focused all my attention. There was something I could do for her: I could make sure I did her credit. There would be reporters, there would be an obituary. I could make sure that the reporters got the facts right—and there were so many marvelous facts to put down. She had already accomplished so much!

"The media will be calling tomorrow," I told Larry, "I'm going to get out Miriam's resume."

I found it easily in her top dresser drawer, several copies

typed and neatly stacked. Studying the dates, the plays, her summer jobs, I was reminded that much of the world perceives "the theater" as an unrealistic luxury. But there was a little-known practical side to it, even for children. If they wanted to audition, if they wanted to perform, they had to put together a resume at a far earlier age than other kids did, because even children's productions require one. Children's Theatre of Annapolis, Annapolis Summer Garden Theater, wherever. Miriam had been updating her resume since she was thirteen. I set one next to our computer to write a one-page biography of her first thing in the morning before I fell mindlessly into bed.

At 6:30 a.m. the shrill ring of the phone pierced my consciousness. I struggled to sit up and listened to the voice calling from overseas.

"Mrs. Rosemary Mild?"

"Yes."

"This is the Scottish police. Are you the mother of Miriam Luby Wolfe?"

"Yes."

"I'm calling about Pan Am Flight 103, ma'am."

My heart stops. Could there have been some mistake? Could it be that she wasn't on it after all?

"I am so sorry, ma'am," the officer's hushed voice said. "There were no survivors."

CHAPTER 4

A House Full, A House Empty

"I PLAN TO SING AND DANCE MY WAY THROUGH LIFE, star on Broadway, become internationally famous, win an Oscar and live happily ever after." These were Miriam's own words from her Severna Park High senior yearbook. Now she was smiling at me from the front page of *The Capital*. The caption under her photo read: "She was a beautiful young woman." My daughter commanded the banner head and lead story. She had become famous all right, but for all the wrong reasons.

We were sitting *shivah,* the traditional days of mourning in a Jewish home. Friends arrived with armfuls of grocery bags and platters. We wouldn't have to cook for a year. Florists delivered arrangements of exquisite lilies and orchids. How could the dead evoke such richesse? I saw these generous gifts as a survival technique—defiant, aggressive symbols of life. The determination to crush the stench and agony of death.

Hundreds of letters and cards began pouring in, many from people I didn't even know. Contributions to charities, some of them totally unfamiliar to me. A peculiar state of mind took up residence in my body. I became a puppet on a string. I fixated on acting the perfect hostess. It served as a defense to falling apart. In our kitchen, three women I hardly knew bustled about, dismantling an opulent basket of fruit. One of the women threw the card in the garbage can under the sink.

31

"Stop!" I said. "I'm in charge here. Don't take things apart or throw anything away. I've lost my daughter, but that doesn't mean I've lost control of my life." I rescued the card. It was from Larry's colleagues at Honeywell! In a spiral notebook I recorded the gift, every gift of food and flowers, every expression of sympathy.

Friends begged Larry and me to let them help and this time I softened. We dispatched them to the airport to pick up our relatives arriving from Wisconsin, New York, Ohio, Minnesota. Another friend rescued us from the anguish of calling the airlines to cancel Miriam's flights to Miami Beach and Syracuse. The phone rang constantly—her friends on the other end; friends who were with her in London calling to tell me how devastated they were. I was so grateful, but I could hardly listen—because they were home safe.

On Christmas Day *The Capital* honored Miriam with a second front page story, "Crash Victim So Full of Life." They published a yearbook picture of her and next to it she had written: "Here I am!" with a smiley face. She was so incredibly happy. I surprised myself by laughing with her.

As I handed out my typed biographical sheets to reporters, I ached with frustration. How to tell them who Miriam really was? How to tell them that trying to set her down on paper was like trying to stuff a tornado into a teacup?

I circulated throughout the house, weaving my way around the relatives and visitors. Our cat and dog were curled up quietly together in a corner. They knew something was terribly wrong. The doorbell rang. Four friends of Miriam's had driven up from Ohio just to attend her memorial service. She had met them at Darien Lake where they were all performing during the summer of '88. Here I was again, the perfect hostess, asking them about their work and families and what shows they were in now. Then I hurried upstairs and dressed as if to attend someone else's funeral, not my only child's.

We arrived at Temple Beth Shalom in a raw, biting cold—a fitting climate. As we walked the path from the parking lot to the sanctuary—Larry almost having to hold me up—I saw in my peripheral vision high school friends of Miriam's I hadn't seen in years; our co-workers; my bosses; and reporters and their cameras, at a respectful distance, for which I was deeply grateful.

Rabbi Klensin's eulogy affected us all.

How bear the unbearable? How comprehend the incomprehensible? Some may find comfort in the idea that it was God's will. But many of us just cannot accept such a theology. No, God's will is that we should live full lives. God wants good people in this world to make the world better, to bring joy, to fight evil. But people have not yet learned to live with each other as God intended. And so a precious young life with so much promise is ended. Yes, even God must be shedding tears over this terrible loss.

We are all aware of Miriam's many achievements in the theater. Many of us saw her act. Many of you performed with her. Her leading roles in Children's Theatre of Annapolis. Serving as president of the Spotlighters at Severna Park High. Receiving an award as best director during One-Act Play Night in her junior year in high school. Winning the Linda Joy Davies Memorial Award for Achievement in the Arts and Humanities in her senior year. Her summer singing and dancing in a show at Darien Lake State Park and the invitation she had received to go back there for a more important role. Her fine work in theater at Syracuse and in London. So many have expressed their confidence that she would have reached the top. Miriam had so many more songs to sing, but that future was not to be.

We have so many beautiful and vivid memories. She was a young girl of seven when my wife and I moved in across the street from Miriam and her family. Watching her grow. Always running, always busy, always smiling. And the memories in this sanctuary. As I stood here with her at Confirmation, asking God's blessing upon her for a full, happy and successful life. And especially the vivid image of Miriam standing right here singing at the wedding ceremony for her mother and Larry. None of us could keep in the tears. But those were tears of joy.

Miriam was an idealist who cared deeply about our world and the pain and suffering of others. She knew it was her responsibility to correct the wrongs of the world. She couldn't understand how others ignore the evil and suffering around them. She expressed this concern as a child collecting for UNICEF and getting others to do so. In London forming a new theater group to bring back to Syracuse that would perform plays on such issues as rape and AIDS. One of her teachers said she responded fully despite any consequences, even to the point of Thoreau-like disobedience. Her grandmother just received a card from her, one of the last Miriam wrote before she died and it contained a quotation from Ghandi: 'The world has enough for every man's need, but not enough for every man's greed.'

Miriam took the time for what was important. She served for two years as co-president of our temple Youth Group and by virtue of that position, as a trustee on our congregational board of directors.

There are so many adjectives we hear to describe Miriam and all of them so true—they are an alphabet of praise and respect. She was affirmative and accomplished, bright and bubbly, creative, caring, charismatic and compassionate, dependable, enthusiastic, friendly and funny, gifted and giving, hurrying, insightful and inspiring, joyous, kind, loving, a listener, motivated and motivating, nurturing, observant, positive, questioning, radiant, sensitive, thoughtful, understanding, vibrant, vital and vivacious.

How can we make sense of this tragedy? We can't. But we must not give victory to those who would destroy life. Miriam wanted to give life. We must carry on for her.

Our response must be to do what she would have done. To help someone; to right a wrong; to raise consciousness; and to smile. To smile, not today nor tomorrow, maybe not next week—it will take awhile. But in time, to smile Miriam's smile for her, to bring some joy. That is what Miriam would have given to us. And as our grief grows dull, to look around and appreciate the world as she would have—as she taught us to do and so she will go on living through us. Miriam will live on through us. *Zecher tzadeket livracha.* The memory of the righteous shall be a blessing.

BACK AT our house, jammed with people after the service, I played my role—considerate of everyone, offering sandwiches. Miriam's Ohio friends put on their jackets. "I have to get back for work," Jody told me. And in the flash of a heartbeat, I assumed her own mother's role: "You have a long trip. Drive carefully, that's the most important thing."

One of our young women visitors handed me a box containing an American flag and a certificate: "This flag was flown over the United States Capitol on December 21, 1988, at the request of the Honorable Henry J. Nowak. This flag will be presented to the parents of Miriam Wolfe." Karen worked for Congressman Nowak, who represented a New York state district including Syracuse.

Contributions poured in from the Jewish National Fund. More than forty trees have been planted in Israel in Miriam's memory. I suddenly remembered a certificate arriving in the mail addressed to "Shane Henry Wolfe"—Miriam's dog. "Dear Sir: A tree has been planted in your honor in the Jewish National Forest in Israel."

"Some day," my daughter once told me, "I'll be able to climb all the trees I want." Looking back, her words seemed to be the beginning of a whole approach to life: that there was nothing in the world she couldn't do—and she started right in! She came home from kindergarten and announced: "Mom, there's going to be a science fair and I'm going to grow an apple tree from a seed."

Was this even possible? I cut open a Red Delicious apple and rustled up half a bag of potting soil from under the sink. She planted the seeds in a small pot. A few weeks later, they sprouted. After the science fair ended, she planted the sprouts in the backyard. A straggly apple tree grew—and even grew bushy. We didn't exactly do it right. It's got a fat, funky sideways trunk. I've since learned that you're supposed to graft a healthy tree cutting onto a newborn one. The tree didn't seem to care. Seven years later, it bore its first apples. I was ecstatic.

"Miriam, you've made yourself immortal!" Little did I know how prophetic I was. But she wasn't much impressed. She was too busy watching *I Love Lucy*. The tree continues to work its magic to this day. When our grandchildren were small, they plucked the apples. Jackie and Myrna baked two pies.

I've discovered a remarkable coincidence: Miriam was born on September 26. And so was John Chapman—better known as Johnny Appleseed, that marvelous pioneer who walked the countryside planting apple trees.

She wrote this poem to her apple tree when she was fifteen. I published it in *Kids' Byline*, February-March issue, 1993.

MY SPECIAL TREE

With each new season I awake
Fom my preoccupation;
And wonder if my tree has changed
Whilst I practiced hibernation.
It's time for my awakening
To see God's gift to me.
Then I stroll out front to my friend,
A very special tree
(Which has many a pleasant memory)
And enjoy a soothingly ecstatic dose
Of God's own gift to me,
My very own special tree.

A majestic maple tree dominated our front yard and sometimes, when Miriam and I had an argument, she'd run outside and I knew just where to find her. I'd look up and there would be two sneakers peeking out through the leaves. She'd be sitting up there, cooling off. Her love of trees lasted her whole life; she even taught a friend to climb one in London.

I stared out the kitchen window at Miriam's bare apple tree silhouetted against the December dusk. As night fell and the house emptied, our exhausted family members bedding down upstairs, I felt the ghostly silence. I moved away from the window. Miriam wasn't coming home. God gave her to me for twenty years. How would I survive without her?

I felt defenseless and deeply threatened. Her plane exploded. I wanted to lash out and wreak vengeance on the powerful evil forces that stole my daughter from me. But who and where was the enemy?

CHAPTER 5

A Pebble in My Pocket

CHRISTMAS DAY. SOMEBODY SWITCHED ON THE TV. Anxious family members clustered in the living room. A cereal commercial blared. Then the kindly face of Charles Kuralt filled the screen. He devoted his program *Sunday Morning* to Pan Am Flight 103, including an interview with a State Department expert on counterterrorism. Suddenly, an amazing thing happened. Mr. Kuralt finished his program with these words:

> It is hard to think of large numbers of disaster victims as individuals, but we should try. We received this letter just before Christmas. It comes to us from Kenneth Bolinsky of Sellersville, Pennsylvania. It says:
> 'Dear Mr. Kuralt:
> In the folklore of Eastern European Jewry is found the tale of the *Tzaddikim*—thirty-six holy good souls upon whose existence lies the responsibility for the balance of good and evil in the universe. The *Tzaddik* is, however, totally unaware of this burden.
> I am writing to tell you of one such soul. During my three years of graduate study at Syracuse University she became a part of my days—a soothing moment in passing. She was a blissfully talented creature full of joy and of light and of love. She was my friend. There is now a serious im-

balance in the universe: Miriam Wolfe was aboard Pan Am Flight 103. I thought you'd want to know.'

OF ALL the passengers on the plane, it was my daughter Mr. Kuralt chose to talk about. I asked myself whether I had understood my child too little; whether I had paid too little attention. In April 1989 I wrote Ken Bolinsky to thank him. Here was his reply:

Dear Mr. and Mrs. Mild:
I got to know Miriam through other friends: I chose to share their grief at her loss, not recognizing my own. We are a strange animal, not always knowing when we have been wounded and, even then, not how deeply. I wrote the letter to Mr. Kuralt out of a sense of fear, of emptiness—I had to share my anxiety. The writing was my catharsis. I cannot tell you why I sent the letter to him—I'm not certain that I know. Perhaps because I have come to trust him. I marked it 'Personal' and never expected a response in any form.

I heard the words I had written while preparing my family's Christmas breakfast and found myself crying again. What followed, though, was something wonderful. As the broadcast made its way across the country, distant friends called to share their frustration at the horror that had befallen us all. Miriam allowed us to touch, and ease, our mutual pain. How like her to help others, to help strangers find a healing peace.

Perhaps that is the memory of your daughter that stays with me: I keep it like a smooth, bright pebble—safe in the bottom of a pocket.

CHAPTER 6

Footprints

"I'M YOUR PAN AM REPRESENTATIVE, ROSEMARY," the deep voice on the phone announced. "Each Flight 103 family has been assigned one."

Miriam had been dead for three days and this was Pan Am's first effort to contact me. And he was calling me by my first name—how dare he?

He talked and I heard noise in the background. "I'm calling you from home," he said. "That's my two-year-old son." (This was not a good beginning.)

"I want to explain to you what's going on in Lockerbie. The Scottish police are in the process of identifying the Flight 103 passengers. What you will need to do, Rosemary, is provide us with documentation to help identify Miriam's body."

Identify Miriam's body. His words ripped through me and a terrible realization set in. At this moment my daughter had no identity at all. I wanted to challenge this Pan Am person, attack him, shout at him: What have you done with her? Where is she now? And what if they can't identify her? But I sealed myself off from my inner hysteria. If I dwelt on these thoughts, I knew I would stop functioning.

On January 2, the doorbell rang. A dark-haired man of medium height stood on our porch.

"FBI Special Agent Robert Saunders." His voice was deferential, yet professional.

A chill shot through me. Even though Larry and I were expecting him, there was something frightening about an official appointment with the Federal Bureau of Investigation. Because Pan Am 103 was an international incident, the FBI was working with the Scottish police and American Consulate in Edinburgh.

Sitting next to him on our living room couch, I could see that Mr. Saunders was a sensitive man who almost felt he was intruding on us. But I knew why he was here. He had come to collect items that might contain Miriam's fingerprints.

He fingerprinted Larry and me so the authorities would be able to distinguish her prints from ours. This act in itself was unnatural—it made me feel like a criminal. The procedure done, I knew what was expected of me and I was prepared. For two days I'd roamed the house asking myself what I could give the FBI that would help identify my child.

All the items I gathered sat before us on the coffee table. They looked so forlorn, so pathetic, almost as if I were invading Miriam's privacy. Trembling, I handed him my treasures. A jar of strawberry jam with a red-flowered calico cover and red yarn ribbon. Miriam made the jam for me that summer at Darien Lake—it was one of my birthday presents. A bottle of her shampoo. Cans of her mousse and shaving cream. A brochure she sent us from King's Head Theatre, where she interned in London. *A Practical Handbook for the Actor*—a gift from a Syracuse faculty member and friend. I also felt compelled to give the agent photographs: Miriam and me in our brown vinyl recliner, where we used to cozily squeeze in together to watch *Dallas* on Friday nights. Three pictures of herself that she'd sent us only two weeks ago. She wore such a joyous smile, with her mass of curls flying in the breeze—against the background of a castle in Wales; a canal and windmills in Amsterdam.

Suddenly, a rush of memory took me back to the hospital in Washington, D.C. where Miriam was born. I remembered a nurse handing me a large white certificate containing my baby's footprints. But would I be able to find it after twenty years? I took

41

the stairs two at a time. And there it was, nestled precisely in the medical folder where I had stored it. But what did I know about a newborn's footprints? Were they the same twenty years later? I didn't even ask Mr. Saunders whether he could use this document—I just had to give it to him. He seemed to understand. "Thank you," he said. "Everything will be returned to you." Our appointment was over.

Days passed in pounding rain and wind-whipped snow. Larry and I wanted answers, we wanted advice, but we did not know who in officialdom to turn to.

The phone rang. "It's the State Department!" Larry shouted. At last! But my first reaction was resentment and anger. Where had my government been all this time? Pan Am 103 exploded over a foreign country. Why wasn't the State Department there for us the night Miriam died? Like Pan Am, the State Department had assigned a liaison to assist each of the families. I got a gentle lady, eager to help, a Ms. Waters.

But peace of mind—in fact, any respite at all—was not to come. My Pan Am representative called again, matter-of-fact and brisk. "The authorities are still working on identifying Miriam's body. Would you please pick up Miriam's dental records from her dentist and orthodontist?"

How could he ask me to do such a thing? And why did they need such records? Wasn't my jar of strawberry jam enough? A wave of nausea overtook me as I visualized myself walking jauntily into their offices: "Hi, there! May I trouble you to hand over my daughter's dental records so her body can be identified?" I grabbed the phone to call Ms. Waters. Her momentary silence told me she was stunned, and then she calmed me.

"Of course, you don't have to do it. You should never have been asked. I will send a courier from the State Department."

"Police Scour Crash Site Like Crime Scene." Within three days they knew it was sabotage: a bomb. My head nearly exploded with questions. How could a bomb have gotten on board? Why didn't Pan Am discover it? What about the Federal Aviation Administration? The FAA was supposed to have strict procedures to prevent a bomb from getting past airport security. Why didn't Pan Am protect my child and the other passengers? Why didn't my government protect them?

Malevolent news stories seeped into the papers. Two weeks before Miriam's plane exploded, our government received a warning that a terrorist attack was to be launched against Pan Am. The attack would take place within a two-week period in December, the approximate time frame of Miriam's flight. Did the government warn Pan Am? And if so, why hadn't Pan Am warned its passengers? My worst nightmare was now confirmed: this calamity could have been prevented.

Sixteen days after Miriam's death, on January 6, I returned to my job at Westinghouse. The engineer for whom I was preparing a briefing sat down next to my desk and opened his briefcase.

"I'm surprised you're back so soon," he said. I consciously pressed my lips together so I wouldn't say something I'd regret. Am I breaking the rules for grieving, sir? Or are you going to invent new ones for me: perhaps *Miss Manners' Guide to Excruciatingly Correct Mourning.*

But I smothered my anger and suppressed my sarcasm as he spread out his papers on my desk. I had come back to work quickly because it was my only salvation. If I had stayed home even one more day, I would have spent every waking moment crying, pacing from room to room; or worse, pacing obsessively in Miriam's room.

But let's be fair. The Westinghouse engineer, a retired Air Force colonel, was not trying to shame me—and deep down I knew it. He was merely trying to express some depth of understanding.

My bosses told me to take as much time off as I needed to. Actually, I would take very little. Being at work gave focus to my life and made me feel worthwhile. As best I could, I compartmentalized myself so I could function and work. Sometimes it helped, often it didn't. In my corner cubicle I gratefully faced the wall, where my designated space provided protection and refuge. But in truth, I wanted to zip myself up into a warm, dark sleeping bag. Head and all. Forever.

I discovered that most of my colleagues felt uncomfortable when I talked about Miriam. They glanced around the room uneasily, hoping I'd stop soon. Dianne was the exception. She listened to me for hours, sometimes with tears in her eyes. She and her husband brought their boys, ages three and eight, to our house for a condolence call. Knowing that their family took many plane trips, I asked her: "Did you tell your kids the truth about how Miriam died?"

"Oh, yes," she said, "I never lie to my children."

In my cubicle I started editing a booklet on the new radar technology to be installed in major U.S. airports. But I couldn't focus. I was still bruised from yesterday—the unavoidable visit to my lawyer's office to take care of official business: Miriam's death certificate. The moment I saw it I wept uncontrollably. The black and white reality of it. Miriam's body was "found December 24." December 24! She was lying out on the cold winter ground in Scotland for three days.

And sitting in the lawyer's office, another reality hit me: I now had to rewrite my will; my family line of inheritance was broken. In our basement storage closet sat cartons that Larry and I had lovingly filled, overflow items from our two households for her first apartment after college.

The phone interrupted. I assumed it was my customer calling about his radar brochure. But no, it was my Pan Am liaison. "I have news, Rosemary. Miriam's body has been identified. It's being shipped to Dulles International Airport in Virginia in two days." I laid down my pencil, grabbed my coat and, without a word, headed for home.

Her father and stepmother went to Dulles to accept Miriam's body. Late that night, Larry and I received it at the funeral home in Annapolis. A gruesome bit of business awaited us. Somebody had to officially identify her. Larry offered, but her father and I agreed it would be unfair for Larry to have to carry that memory with him.

Rabbi Klensin came to the rescue. After making the identification, he told us, "Yes, it's Miriam, but you don't want to see her." I took his word for it.

At the funeral home we chose the coffin, a burnished walnut, and I sat down in a corner to reflect. Several times during her college years, Miriam quoted this little poem by Zoe Atkins:

> So much do I love wandering,
> So much I love the sea and sky,
> That it will be a piteous thing
> In one small grave to lie.

WHAT prompted Miriam to cite this poem so often? Was it a terrible premonition? Life was so precious to her and now, lifetimes before her time, she lay in a piteous grave.

Not many teenagers give a thought to how the hereafter will remember them. They think themselves invincible—they're gonna live forever. In Miriam's Honors English class at Severna Park High, students were asked to describe the tombstone they would want for themselves and write their epitaph. At age fifteen, this is what she said:

My tombstone will be a very large monument where the public can have access to it. It will be right outside the Metropolitan Opera House and a fresh supply of red roses will be a prominent sight every day. The monument will become a landmark. My epitaph will read "Miriam Wolfe was a true performer. She could transport those in the audience to another time and place, if they just believed in her and in themselves. She will remain clear in our memories Forever."

ON JANUARY 9, 1989, huddled together at the synagogue cemetery, our two tortured families met for a private burial. We chose a fitting epitaph for the headstone: "She was blissfully talented, full of joy, light and love"—from Ken Bolinsky's letter to Charles Kuralt.

We laid her to rest next to Larry's first wife on a grassy hillside not 100 yards from the original site of the Charter Oak, a historic Annapolis landmark. The cemetery was kitty-corner to Annapolis Mall.

"Maybe this is the right location," I told Larry. "Miriam loved to shop."

Jewish tradition has it that you place a pebble on the grave you've come to visit. A few months later at Miriam's grave, Larry and I discovered a stuffed Snoopy, dressed in corduroy railroad overalls. Sure enough, in the front pocket, we found a large pebble. I remembered Ken Bolinsky's poignant reference to Miriam as a "pebble in a pocket."

We have no idea who left Snoopy, so we carried him home to shelter him from the elements. Many months later, I coaxed a confession from a modest Tara Ungar, a gifted writer and high school friend of Miriam's who visited her grave often, leaving poems, stuffed animals and messages.

A few weeks later, the following letter, written by Tara, appeared at the grave.

Dear Mr. Murderer:

I just wanted to drop you a line and see how you were doing. How are your children? Do you listen adoringly as they chime about their day at school, or about how much they love you? My friend's mother will never again hear the sweet, excited voice telling her of the triumphs and joys in life. And your wife? Does she bring you all the joy and love my friend never had a chance to give? Mr. Murderer, let me tell you—she was full of love, light and joy. She touched everyone she met, giving them a special gift that few have been chosen to give. And when your children cry at night? Do you hold them in your arms? Does your charming way soothe their fears, ease the tender hearts? No one comforted my friend seconds before your filthy bomb took her from this world. From those who loved her. From those she would have loved. And when her broken body met the earth, were you dancing with your soul mate? Were your children asleep in their beds? Far removed from horrors? From barbarism? When they look into your eyes, do they see the fire? The death? When your little girl slips from your lap is there blood on your hands? Does it soak through the delicate lace dress? Does the stench make you ill? Because you are drenched with blood. I could damn you to Hell, or curse your innocent children, Mr. Murderer, but I won't. I condemn you to live a painfully long life—to stare despondency and emptiness in the face, to lie in bed with fear, grief and loss and to walk hand in hand forever with tragedy and inconsolability. And when you glance over your shoulder each day, may your unspeakable crimes sting your eyes and burn in your ears.

CHAPTER 7

The Room Where She Lives

IT WILL ALWAYS BE MIRIAM'S ROOM, a room full of irrefutable evidence that she once lived, loved and made a difference on this earth. The decor she selected still delights me: lime green and lemon yellow and one wall of wild rabbits romping in daisies. Seven-foot-tall bookcases overflow with books and *tchotchkes*—music boxes, candles, china animals. Art prints grace the walls: Renoir's *Luncheon of the Boating Party*, Picasso's *Don Quixote* and an Andrew Wyeth *Helga* portrait.

Sitting down at her desk (which she merely piled high with stuff and never once used for studying), I open a leather photo album to a fading shot of a clapboard Cape Cod with wraparound porch: the house where Miriam was born. My first husband, Jim Wolfe, and I relocated from New York City to this College Park, Maryland, house when he took a position with the federal government. For the first month we whispered, then suddenly woke up: "Hey, we're not in an apartment anymore."

The move cost me my job as an assistant editor at *Harper's Magazine*, and at age thirty-two I found myself applying for the role of motherhood. On September 26, 1968, six-pound two-ounce Miriam burst into our world. She arrived twelve days early, already in a hurry. We spent the rest of her life running behind her trying to catch up.

The moment she was placed in my arms, I anxiously gave her the once-over: a mat of light brown hair, scrunched up little face, perfect tiny fingers and toes. Oh and a large nose, but that was okay—so was mine.

A steel bar connects her baby shoes At two months her feet were noticeably pigeon-toed. The pediatrician prescribed special shoes, forcing her feet outward. Laced into the shoes for the first time, she howled in protest—but not for long. She began entertaining herself by lying on her back, raising her tiny thin legs like a weight-lifter, pumping iron at three months. Soon she was flipping over, hopping about the house like a bunny. At six months the special shoes came off. Still she continued to hop on both knees. I had read that crawling was an essential stage in learning to read, so I got down on the floor and pushed her knees one after the other. In a few minutes she got the idea.

Our new home in Severna Park, Maryland—a four-bedroom colonial. The neighborhood teemed with toddlers and Jim liked being near the water—between two scenic tributaries of the Chesapeake Bay, the Severn and the Magothy, just eight miles north of historic Annapolis.

The suburban silence of Severna Park took a little getting used to: like landing in the Sahara Desert after eight years in New York City. But as I pushed the stroller down Kennedy Drive, I began to revel in the luxury of full-time motherhood. Miriam was turning out to be the most interesting person I'd ever met. At two-and-a-half, she started developing an uncanny intuition. Early one morning she studied her father as he rushed out to the car, facing a new job with a long commute. Sensing his anxiety, she called to him from the front door: "Daddy, get along with people!"

Page after page of toddler photos in our fenced backyard. Shortly after sending her out to play, I heard a gentle knock at the back door. I didn't respond soon enough. A much louder, more desperate knock followed. "Mommy, let me in. It's Miriam, your child."

Miriam standing teary-eyed with her teacher—waving

goodbye to me on her first day of nursery school. Weeks later, I learned that she'd been crying every day.

"Do you let Miriam dress herself?" her teacher asked at our first conference. Confused, I shook my head. "Let her," the teacher urged. "It'll help her become more independent."

The next day Miriam chose her own clothes. I gritted my teeth as I dropped her off in her misbuttoned red jacket, pink suede oxfords and red tights *sans* skirt. On a field trip with her class three weeks later, the teacher whispered to me: "We love the way Miriam dresses herself. We can't wait to see what she'll wear next." The tactic worked; her crying stopped, her confidence grew and in time, her outfits even matched.

As much as I loved motherhood, I missed my career. I found a compromise, a copy editing position with Williams & Wilkins, a large medical and scientific publisher in Baltimore. Best of all, I could work at home. I brought Miriam with me to pick up a new assignment. Fifty women copy editors and only two men bent over their desks.

My three-year-old sized up the place in a shrill baby voice: "There are too many ladies here."

A fortyish single co-worker responded: "You got that right, Miriam."

At age eight sitting up in a hospital bed. Sitting up indeed. She had been sedated prior to surgery to remove a cyst from inside her cheek—evidently not sedated well enough. She rode the gurney down the hall to the OR bolt upright, waving to nurses and other patients.

"What are you doing up?" the astonished oral surgeon asked. Just my daughter not wanting to miss anything.

Miriam engrossed in her newest stack of library books. So often she reminded me of those Early American primitive paintings that portrayed small children as miniature grownups. She seemed to have been born with an adult sense of purpose. She inherited this trait from my mother, a journalist and author, who fought through decades of illness to accomplish a lifetime in forty-eight years. "Do it now while it's fresh" she often admonished my brother and me. This sense of urgency propelled Miriam, too; the intensity infused her whole life.

A glass jar filled with fifty sharks' teeth. We discovered the teeth in the sand on our family vacation to the Outer Banks of North Carolina. Back home, I called the Smithsonian Institution. A kindly paleontologist invited us to his office, identified them for us, and Miriam glued them onto poster board for a first-grade science fair. In succeeding years, the science fairs awarded her prizes for "A Trip through a Cow's Stomach"; "How a Telephone Works" (with tin cans and string); "Turning Rocks into Jewelry"; and in sixth grade, "How Alcohol Affects the Body," which netted her a countywide third place, a gold medal and a $25 check.

Twelve years later, I happened to tell a colleague of mine about our sharks' teeth. But I wished afterward that I'd kept my mouth shut. He turned on me, bass voice booming: "My wife and I just spent a week at Nag's Head and we didn't find a single one. You and Miriam took them all!"

She sprawls on the floor amid her Barbies. On a summer day in her eighth year, Miriam emptied the small suitcase that held her Barbie clothes, filled it with a few of her own and started down the stairs. Encountering me in the front hall, she stopped and declared, "I'm running away. Talk me out of it."

I did. But then I took her in my arms and asked her why she wanted to run away. Tears flooded her azure blue eyes and she hid her curly blonde head in my chest.

"Because you and Daddy argue so much," she whispered.

A shot of the three of us in front of the house. No one is smiling. Even the absence of smiles couldn't reveal the extent of the turmoil overtaking our little family. After two decades as an editor, I bolted from my introverted profession and became a real estate agent. But I'd never worked on straight commission before. How did anyone pay the mortgage in this business?

I had to learn fast. My husband and I lived in a boating paradise and owned two small sailboats, but there were no calm waters at our house. Our marriage was headed for the rocks. Perhaps it was inevitable. We had gravitated to each other as complete opposites, but the charm eventually wore off. On New Year's Eve, 1977, while the rest of the world sipped champagne, Jim and I bitterly slammed doors and shouted our angry goodbyes. Goodbye to seventeen years of marriage.

As I return this album to its place, my eye catches a title on the shelf above. Shortly after Miriam died, I discovered a yellow scrap of paper among her college notebooks. On it she'd written: "Show Mom p. 60 of *The Road Less Traveled.*" Trembling, I opened the book. Page 60 criticized parents who think they're protecting their children by hiding the truth:

"Such protection is unsuccessful. The children know anyway that Mommy and Daddy had a fight the night before. . . .The result then is not protection but deprivation. . . .[The children] are deprived of role models of openness and honesty."

Miriam was nine when her father and I separated. She and I got to keep the house—her life's continuity being foremost in all our minds. We spent many tearful hours talking about divorce, but mostly she cried and begged, "You can get back together, if you only try." She made up a game to act out the reconciliation: Barbie and Ken Get Married. I took her to a Parents Without Partners picnic, launching into the ugly business of meeting new men. On the way home she complained: "Mom, you were flirting!" Her frustration turned confrontational, I yelled a lot, and we entered the year of living disastrously.

A photo of Miriam on her knees, hugging her dog. I take a deep breath and run my tongue over my lips. Within six months of my separation, all six of our pets—Shane (the dog), Cuddles (the kitten), Teeny and Tiny (the two gerbils) and two anonymous goldfish—ascended to pet heaven. Had I put a hex on them? I doubt it, but perhaps our misery infected them and they all just decided to call it quits. Still, I couldn't help but think I'm a terrible mother!

Years later, Miriam admitted to me: "I hated your marriage." And therein lay the ambivalence for us both. We found it so hard to face up to the end of the dream, the stereotype of the happy family. But the conflicts in our home had been so intense that within weeks of my separation, relatives and friends told me: "You and Miriam are so much more relaxed now."

Shots of Miriam as she played with her brand-new kitten. I rewarded her for making the honor role. Another pet—would I never learn? He sat poised atop an end table in our living room. With his glowing yellow eyes and Buddha posture, he looked like the last accessory the decorator had set down. Hoppy mastered kitchen cabinets and refrigerator doors. No Froot Loops box escaped his raids. When he got bellyaches, Miriam tried to spoon-feed him Pepto Bismol, which he firmly declined, of course. So she dribbled it across his paws and he frantically licked them clean. Success!

A picture of Miriam and me, a stack of Multiple Listing printouts under my arm. Two-and-a-half years of selling houses and the roller-coaster income just about did me in. The final straw: I discovered there was no such thing as a reliable baby-sitter who was also a wallflower and always available evenings and weekends. Even taking Miriam along on my appointments didn't work. She tried to be helpful. But not all buyers were charmed by my ten-year-old running up the stairs ahead of us, calling out: "Wait till you see the master bedroom!"

I returned to the Baltimore publishing house to edit medical books and journals. I put in twenty-one hours in the office to get benefits and twenty more at home to raise my daughter in peace and good conscience.

Music to my ears. A piano teacher who came to our house after school—how great was that? I recruited three neighbor kids for back-to-back lessons after Miriam's, allowing me to spend extra time at my job. The kids played in our backyard before and after their lessons. Little did the teacher know she was doubling as my sitter for two hours each week.

Five laughing little girls waving from the windows of

my Chevy Chevette. Carpool time. My new life could have been solitary and self-pitying. But Miriam did something for me that nobody else could have done: she brought purpose and a sense of community to my world. I always found a reason to be somewhere, to be doing something—helping with homework or class projects, getting her to religious school, the library, Girl Scouts and softball. I became fast friends with some of her friends' parents. Yeah, I carpooled my brains out. And sometimes I went overboard playing supermom.

Many times I should have been willing to learn from her. The Chevette turned out to be a lemon. I drove it 110,000 miles, enduring outrageous repair expenses. Miriam kept saying, "Mom, get rid of it!" I kept not listening.

She also had big plans for me socially. A mischievous look, hiding something behind her back. It was a letter she'd neatly print-ed to gorgeous Howard Keel, my favorite actor on *Dallas*, inviting him to our house for cocktails—and signed my name. I wasn't dat-ing and she thought I needed a little boost. I wouldn't let her mail it. Hey, maybe I should have.

Miriam and her friend Shannon playing dress-up. Shan-non's mother referred to her daughter as "My Shannon," and I liked that, so I spoke of Miriam to a friend on the phone in the same way. She overheard me.

"I am not your Miriam," she retorted. "I'm eleven years old and I don't belong to anyone. I'm my own person." Oooookay.

I had often felt my marital identity depended on my lobster Cantonese and veal scaloppini. After we separated: "Hey! I don't have to do that anymore." I retired from gourmet cooking—big time.

"Mom?" Miriam asked timidly one night, "Do you think we could have something for dinner that doesn't come in a box?"

But when I did make the effort, I'd brown the beef and chop, chop, chop to create an overflowing platter of the tacos she loved—and she'd eat one. "It's delicious, Mom, but I'm full." She ate six bird-like meals a day, never gained any weight, never went over 112 pounds; her rocket-like energy just burned it away.

A shot of Miriam with the telephone at her ear—an extension of her anatomy. In junior high, two major influences dominated her life: the telephone and *General Hospital*. At 9:30 one evening I returned home from a meeting and found our sitter greeting me at the door, ashen-faced. Miriam was calling MGM in Hollywood, trying to reach her favorite *GH* actress. "Get off the phone this minute!" I yelled.

Thirteenth birthday—a slumber party. Sleeping bags wall-to-wall in the living room. Early the next morning, I came downstairs to find ten girls sprawled on the floor building Legos.

Every week we watched the TV show *Fame.* It planted the seed for a life in the theater. As soon as the theme song came on, Miriam would leap up from the couch to sing and dance along. "Fame—I'm gonna live forever, I'm gonna learn how to fly." She'd throw herself into the frenzied jazz beat, becoming part of the music. At those moments, I too thought she would live forever.

She actually had the opportunity to visit the set of *Fame* in California and mingle with the actors. She darted up to Valerie Lansburg:

"Can I have your autograph?" Miriam asked.

"Sure."

"You're my favorite actress."

"Oh, not me, it should be someone like Glenda Jackson."

"You have a marvelous singing voice, it's beautiful. But you smoke!"

"That's what someone just said to me. I'm grown up. I have a right to smoke."

"Oops, sorry! It was nice meeting you."

"Nice meeting you, too."

With clenched teeth I often wondered whether I would survive seventh grade. Shortly after entering Severna Park Junior High, my sweet little kid turned mouthy, aggressive and challenging—for a lot of reasons. Leaving nurturing Folger McKinsey Elementary for a school of a thousand students. Puberty and its hormones. Parents divorced, no father in the house to back me up. And a nasty older girl on the school bus who harassed her daily. I had to concoct a written excuse about after-school care to get her switched to a different bus.

Miriam's trip to California was to visit her grandparents, Bert and Joe Wolfe. Her best friend, Wendy, accompanied her; I wouldn't have let her go alone. But when she returned, she told me a few things I really didn't want to hear. A flight attendant had asked for their drink order. "A martini!" Miriam chirped. Relating this, she burst into giggles. But then her face turned somber. "Grandma and Grandpa liked Wendy better than me."

Practicing her clarinet. During her band concerts, she had a look of such joy when she played, I envied her. But the climax of the year turned into a dud. The band members were treated to a dinner theater, but Miriam didn't return her permission slip on time. She wasn't allowed to go. I wrote the band teacher a note, begging for mercy. No deal. A tough lesson in responsibility, which I took more seriously than she did. She just shrugged it off.

Piano and clarinet gave way to voice lessons. Even untrained, her soprano voice had a sweet, vibrant, resonant tone. On her own, at thirteen, she located a professional opera singer/teacher, who accepted her as a student. Four months after beginning the technically demanding voice lessons, she landed her first role—for Children's Theatre of Annapolis. She played the prissy Mrs. Purdy in *Forty-Five Minutes from Broadway*. Thus began several beautiful years with CTA, during which she performed five leading and major roles.

Another playbill: *Snow White and the Seven Dwarfs of the Black Forest*. Miriam played Queen Bella in that spoof of the fairy tale.

Children in the audience screamed at Snow White, "Don't bite the apple!"

Queen Bella leaned menacingly over the edge of the stage to the littlest ones down front. "Shut up, my dears," she ad-libbed. The children loved it.

But sometimes her nerves got to her. She auditioned for Annapolis Summer Garden Theater's production of *Brigadoon*. An intimidating setting for a fourteen-year-old: a smoke-filled room crowded with experienced adult actors and dancers and a three-hour wait for her turn. Her warmed-up voice cooled down. The director thought she sang just fine, but she didn't think so. Next came the dance tryout. She rushed from the line in tears—in the middle of the routine—prompted by the difficult choreography. She even refused the resulting callback. Too embarrassed.

On the third shelf sits *Familiar Quotations* by John Bartlett—with at least a dozen of Miriam's Post-its still peeking out of its pages. I gave her the new edition on her sixteenth birthday. My mother had given me a copy in high school and it was time to pass on the legacy. Miriam embraced it as if she'd been waiting for it her whole life. She bought blank books intended as diaries, and on randomly scattered pages, she copied germane quotes in calligraphy and gave the books as gifts.

In the one she gave me, the quotes include: "I cannot and will not cut my conscience to fit this year's fashions" (Lillian Hellman); and on the very last page, Daniel Webster's deathbed words: "I still live." For the rest of my days I will wonder why she chose that quote.

A CTA playbill for *Joseph and the Amazing Technicolor Dreamcoat*. After performing the role of co-narrator, she wrote for Honors English:

> I feel an incredible sense of delight. The most delightful feeling I have ever experienced was the sudden rush of applause and an audience of 700 simultaneously standing. It goes on and on and on and I feel so thrilled I want to burst. A standing ovation and continuous applause are the ultimate forms of approval.

An *Arundel Sun* photograph of Miriam and her camp-

ers at London Town Publick House, south of Annapolis. Now a national museum with rolling lawns and wooded gardens on the South River, it served as a bustling seaport 300 years ago. I had taken an afternoon off to drive her to the interview for a camp counselor job, and as I waited in the car, feelings of tenderness and pride almost overwhelmed me. She looked so dignified in her blue suit and white blouse, yet she radiated an innocent charm. As she slid back into the car, she smiled and announced: "I got the job."

She worked at this Living History camp for three summers, re-creating colonial life for children. They made corn husk dolls; studied history and architecture; cooked a pioneer meal on the hearth; wove baskets; and dyed cloth from plants. This experience brought her to another great love in her life: teaching. She became friends with another counselor, Dina McPherson, who happened to be the psychology teacher at Severna Park High. Twenty years later, their paths would cross in a truly eerie and unexpected way.

A drama club program for Severna Park High's One-Act Play Night. Miriam entered the competition as a director and chose *Impromptu*, a psychological play. Twenty-five auditioned for the three parts, including one of her close friends. The friend didn't get the part—she wasn't right for it. But Miriam managed to soothe any ruffled feathers and keep the friendship. She also won the award for Best Director and one of her performers won for Best Actress.

Underlying this heady experience lurked the anxiety of choosing a college. She had already chosen her career, musical theater. Was I happy about it? Heavens, no. We discussed the hazards. That is, I harangued. She pirouetted around her room.

I recited my well-rehearsed arguments. You're only as good as your last part. Most actors are unemployed most of the time. The theater attracts, by its very nature, a disproportionate number of petty, clawing, cutthroat, unstable people.

She knew all that. On her vanity sat two framed photos, one of Judy Garland and one of Joan Crawford.

"Dear," I said, trying not to whine, "are these women role

models for you? They were so neurotic and had such messed-up lives."

"They were fine artists, Mom," she said, executing an arabesque. "You know, I don't have to become a Mommy Dearest."

I had to laugh, but I wasn't quite finished. "I didn't encourage you to become an actress."

"Oh no? You and Dad had me performing for your friends from the time I was six!"

A well-researched, polished article in *The Capital*, "Greasy Kidstuff." As president of the Drama Club, Miriam wrote it with her friend Jennifer in a crusade against censorship. Severna Park High refused to let the Spotlighters perform *Grease* because "it contains sex, booze and rock and roll."

"Can you believe it?" Miriam said. "They don't understand that the play's a satire." But the club members did persuade the principal to add a student to the adult committee that made those decisions. Ten years after her crusade, the high school finally performed *Grease*.

Prom night. If there's such a thing as Promzilla, she qualified. Throwing a hissy fit in a dressing room over a too-big crinoline. Pleading for an expensive makeover at Annapolis Mall (I caved). Prom night, at sunset on the lawn at a friend's home, the couples posed for pictures in *Great Gatsby* splendor—Miriam in white taffeta with a pink satin bow. This romantic scene came a day after she begged her date, "Please bring your father's car." The week before, she'd gotten trapped in the seatbelt of Matt's junker and he'd had to cut her out of it with scissors. The host parents invited me into their living room and offered me a canapé: a cracker heaped with black caviar. I instantly dropped it upside down on their white carpet. Oh yeah, my daughter and I made quite a pair that week. At 2:30 a.m., she waltzed into the house and plunked herself down on my bed, giggling nonstop during her blow-by-blow account of the evening.

"Mom, we ended up walking on the Chartwell Country Club golf course. I stood there and asked myself, 'What am I doing here?'"

"Do you mean the golf course or the whole experience?"

"The whole thing."

Her Andrew Wyeth Helga print catches my eye. One weekend when my father was visiting, Miriam raced down the stairs to breakfast and burst upon us.

"You've got to come with me to see the Helga paintings," she said breathlessly. She'd already been to the National Gallery show twice. I was skeptical.

"Won't it be boring, a whole exhibit on just one subject?"

"No. I want so much to share it with you. You won't be disappointed, I promise." And we weren't. Grandpa Saul, Larry and I were exhilarated. She led us through the rooms like an experienced docent and later wrote notes of her impressions:

Wyeth's paintings are hypnotizing and endlessly varied. Helga's plain, sturdy clothes—earnest grays and browns, painted with such exquisite detail you can almost touch the fabric. Sunlight sweeping into a window, ambushing a stark room. Brooding shadows falling on a winter tree. Helga in the fetal position on a bed, with only a bare bulb illuminating her desolate world.

A photo of father and daughter. A three-pack-a-day smoker, her dad had just quit. Miriam had been begging him to quit for years, bombarding him with literature she'd ordered from the American Lung Association. When he developed a hearing problem, she promptly contacted Miracle Ear; she'd seen their TV commercials. For years afterward, Miracle Ear brochures filled our mailbox.

On Senior Awards Night she received the Linda Joy Davies Award for Achievement in the Arts and Humanities, an engraved silver bowl; a one-time award in memory of a student killed in a car accident.

Four excellent colleges accepted her, including Syracuse, her first choice, where she had to audition in New York for the drama department. Despite accolades and acceptances, she stormed about the house, short-tempered and edgy. I assumed it was her anxiety at losing her familiar high school comfort zone to tackle the great unknown ahead. Days later, she confessed, "I was so worried about our two families being together at graduation." Sadly, graduation night Miriam and the Wolfes went for their afterward treat and separately, my father and I went for ours. How ironic that since her death we have all gotten along just fine.

In front of her dorm, trying hard to look cheerful. Her eighteenth birthday fell on the Friday of Parents Weekend and I eagerly flew up. What a disaster. She cried the whole weekend. The school had squeezed her and two roommates into a double—a room so tiny they couldn't even use one of the desks; they had to stack it on top of another one just to be able to walk around. I had brought a birthday cake sporting yellow roses, but where to set it down? I had to hold it on my lap. The dorm reminded me of Animal House. Thundering humanity, no privacy, no way to quietly study or practice voice lessons. Heavy drinking. "You can't even go into the bathroom on weekends, Mom, everybody's throwing up."

And the intensity of the drama department took some getting used to. When she wasn't doing research for the production of *Hamlet,* she was mopping the stage till midnight. She learned the craft of lighting the hard way. "I pulled the wrong lever and the whole stage went dark. The audience roared. It wasn't funny, Mom."

She wrote to a high school teacher: "For the most part, I'm happy. The drama department is full of talented, dedicated people. But because all of the actor's work is based on self, it's easy to lose our perspective as to who we really are. I always thought I had a good sense of self, but now I'm not so sure. I only know that I'm a very different person from when I left."

Sitting on our front porch, radiant in a fuchsia turtleneck and jeans. She wrote in her journal about coming home for Thanksgiving:

As the station wagon swings past the entrance to my community, my heart beats in anticipation. The maple tree that brushes its leaves against my bedroom window is the first thing framed in the car window. I am home at last. As I squint, I recognize that orange and white lump in the middle of the yard. My cat yawns, as if to say, "I'm glad you're home, but I'm too proud to show it." Now the car is pulling into the driveway and I open the door before it stops rolling. I sprint across the yard, take the front porch steps all in one leap and run smack into my mother. She and I laugh and hug each other as my dog runs in circles around us. Midnight greets me with a kiss and I stroke her soft fur. A feeling of warmth envelops me and suddenly my life is in perspective again. I am safe, warm and loved.

THAT NIGHT I introduced my daughter to my new boyfriend, Larry. As she and I were getting ready for bed, I said: "Larry's really romantic. What do you think of him?"

"I think you should marry him," she promptly answered.

By the end of her freshman year, he and I were engaged and we drove up to Syracuse to bring her home. We found her with only half a suitcase packed amid a Mount Everest of clothes, books, tapes, stereo speakers and makeup.

"Miriam," I said, "we need a Roadway semi." And was she testy with us. We were interfering with her goodbyes to her friends. In a pounding rain, Larry tied down the open trunk lid with rope—no way could we close it—and Scotch-taped plastic trash liners around the Honda's hindside. We stuffed Miriam into the few empty inches of the back seat for the seven-hour drive home in the nonstop downpour without benefit of rear view mirror.

New car, new job. My father bought me a Toyota Corolla to celebrate my new job as an engineering writer for Westinghouse. It meant a higher salary, better benefits and a shorter commute, but lots of overtime. Now there was less of me available for both

Miriam and Larry.

She, of course, was having a tough time adjusting to us; she'd had her mother all to herself for nine years. When I accepted Larry's proposal of marriage, I assumed she was comfortable with it. But I couldn't have been more wrong. A change came over her. So subtle I hardly noticed. Or I didn't want to notice. I was so wrapped up in my job, trying to prove myself, plus the spooky prospect of remarrying, that I neglected to ease the way for my only child.

Three weeks after our first date, Larry invited me to join him on a two-week trip to Hawaii. "You can come as my bride if you want."

Had I heard right? Hawaii, yes! Marriage, I wasn't ready. In fact, I wasn't even ready for constant closeness. "I need my space," I protested over the next several months.

Larry didn't understand. "What's spooky? Why do you need space?" He's a man with a firm vision for himself, whatever his goal, whether it's cleaning the basement or writing a novel. Or choosing a bride. Once he fixes on it, he surges ahead and never looks back.

Truth be told, I knew the minute I met him that he was The One—in fact, fifteen minutes before he even stepped into the front hall. Our first date was for six o'clock. I dressed early and happened to look out the window at 5:45. He had already arrived and was sitting in his car reading a newspaper. Apparently, he wasn't going to ring the bell early in case I wasn't ready. Wow! So considerate! We hit it off perfectly. I'm sure we knew each other in a previous life.

A portrait of pain. Eight months after our blind date, we announced our engagement. During SU spring break, Miriam brought us a gift. It was a portrait of her, twelve by thirteen inches, done by an artist friend and classmate.

The unframed oil painting shocked me. The aggressive brush strokes revealed a somber, haunted expression. This wasn't the exuberant daughter who sang and pirouetted throughout our house. The artist captured what I had stubbornly refused to recognize: that Miriam felt threatened. She had not yet comprehended that she was gaining a kindly stepfather and two loving new sisters. All she could think of was that she was losing her mother.

Years after her death, we learned about a disturbing remark Miriam had made to Laura, one of her roommates. She had a strange feeling she wasn't going to live very long.

During our engagement, Larry undertook the labors of Hercules: working long days as an engineer at Honeywell; packing up his own house of twenty-nine years to move into ours; and remodeling our basement. Talk about a challenge. Our basement was one huge cluttered space. He spent nights and weekends transforming it into four paneled rooms: a Ping Pong room, extra bedroom, furnace room, laundry room and two huge closets. He'd spend several nights a week at our house. Once when we'd gone to bed early, Miriam, in a manic mood, put the sensual Ravel's *Bolero* on the stereo and turned the volume up to deafening.

"Is she doing that for our benefit?" Larry asked me. Of course, she was. We ignored her, but I was mortified.

Part of Miriam's distress at our engagement involved her yearning to have a serious boyfriend of her own. In a letter to a friend, she wrote: "Mom and Larry are sickeningly cute together and in love. How I envy them." Many men were interested in her, but a real relationship hadn't gelled yet. In her journal freshman year, she wrote about the young man she was dating at SU. "He's so possessive—and we haven't even gotten to know each other yet. He wants to have a girlfriend. He wants her to belong to him, whereas I want to be with someone, to enjoy and appreciate each other."

Larry and I were married at Temple Beth Shalom on Thanksgiving weekend of Miriam's sophomore year. We came out of the rabbi's study and stood at the back. Miriam, seated next to my father in the front row, stood, faced us and sang "Unexpected Song" from Andrew Lloyd Webber's *Song and Dance*. The lyrics describe a truly unexpected love. In her vibrant soprano voice, so fresh and bell-like, she sang just to us and for us.

On that day Miriam acquired her two stepsisters. And because both are gifted art teachers and artists—Jackie a sculptor, Myrna a ceramist and print-maker—the three new sisters forged an immediate bond that reached beyond love to creativity.

After a lunch during winter break with her three best friends from high school, Miriam wrote in her journal:

> It was so nice to know that, despite the fact that our lives are different now, we can still relate to one another. I've never felt better than I did at that luncheon—so secure, so peaceful, so at ease with being me. It's a good thing, too, because the drama department was beginning to make me wonder. At Bay Country theater camp I was taught to "always be sincere in your own life. There are lots of artificial actressy types and they get in trouble because they don't know what's real any more. If you feel insecure, be insecure, etc." At home, I'm real, I've earned the right to be real. At school the same thing must happen.

I find a playbill from SU's production of *Anne of Green Gables*. The *Syracuse Post-Standard* said: "Wonderfully fresh and entertaining. Fine characterizations. Miriam Wolfe played Mrs. Spencer as a muddled Mrs. Malaprop with a shrill voice and fluttering mannerisms."

Larry and I drove up to Syracuse to see her in the play *Woyzeck*, an allegory of mob psychology. A fellow cast member gave her a note before opening night: "You are a very intelligent, incredible human being. Don't be so hard on yourself!"

A playbill of Woody Allen's *Don't Drink the Water* for the Pasadena (Maryland) Theatre Company. In June after sophomore year, she won the role of the ingenue Susan Hollander. The male lead, a seasoned actor twice her age, wrote her a note. "By observing the way you 'slide into' a character: experimenting, choosing role models, changing attitudes and inflections; and by watching you on stage whenever possible: movements, gestures, poses, etc.—from these observations I have been able to apply many new ideas to my own character and to my acting in general. It has really helped. For that I want to thank you."

WHEN SHE wasn't on stage, she revealed more personal preoccupations in her journal.

> *Don't Drink the Water* opened tonight and I feel I gave a good solid performance. Now that I have to do love scenes, that's one hurdle I'm over. I just wish that the only heavy-duty kissing I've ever been involved with wasn't because I'm in a show. All I know is I want to get over this preoccupation with my sexuality. I want to lose my virginity! There, I've said it! I feel like half a woman, a mutant. But it's got to be with the right guy.
>
> My date last night with David was wonderful. The Annapolis Brass Quintet played beautifully. At the Chart House we chatted over tea and mud pies and then drove back to his house. We talked from eleven o'clock on. Finally he put his arm around me. So we ended up lying on the couch the entire night. (Talk about taking a risk!) It was so nice; someone twenty-three, attractive, intelligent, who finds me both his intellectual equal and physically attractive. How nice to lie there while he stroked my hair and back and just TALK! Things like this always happen when you don't look for them. Too bad he lives so far away now. I didn't want a long distance relationship, but it looks like I've no choice. Well, there certainly are worse things!

A WEEK into summer vacation, she sang in a friend's wedding and donated her 300 stuffed animals to the YWCA battered spouse shelter. Then, oops . . . As Larry and I came in from a weekend in St. Louis, I heard a tearful, trembling voice calling from the kitchen.

"Mom! I had an accident in the Naval Academy parking lot. I hit a Mercedes! The midshipman said it was a graduation present from his dad." Then she cheered herself up. "At least it was a used Mercedes."

The bright-red scrapbook from Darien Lake. She auditioned for and landed a summer job singing and dancing at Darien Lake, the largest theme park in New York State. Three days after she got there, she wrote to her friend Jessica:

I have to learn twenty-four songs and the choreography in six days. I don't know if I can do it. I'm on an emotional roller coaster. Today I burst into tears out of frustration. But every time I get discouraged, I think of what you told me—how good this'll be for me and how it'll cure my stage fright. I have five numbers where I dance with someone from the audience. When I first started learning the choreography for "Material Girl," I thought: This is sexy stuff— they must be thinking of someone else! But I'm getting it!

A photo of us at Darien Lake. I visited her for a long weekend to celebrate my birthday while Larry was in England on business and she showered me with surprises. A Happy Birthday banner; two pairs of earrings, gold and silver; three jars of strawberry jam she had made in the kitchen of the family she was living with; plus cheese, crackers and fruit, all carefully wrapped in a straw basket. That night she stayed with me at Holiday Inn and we talked till 3 a.m. The next day I learned what it was like to be totally immersed in show biz.

"Backstage" was a tiny cubbyhole and the routines were grueling. But they were also delightful. I sat through six shows and loved every minute. Miriam and two other singers, plus a lively backup band, comprised *The Heart of Rock and Roll*, with songs from the Fifties to the Eighties. And sure enough, by performing thirty-two shows a week, she got over her stage fright.

"What do you do between shows?" I asked her.

"Sometimes we color," she said, pointing to her large pile of coloring books and crayons. Which didn't surprise me. At Syracuse she'd bought herself a Mr. Potato Head.

During my visit, we sat at a picnic table and talked—at one point, about my divorce.

"I didn't start growing up until I got divorced," I told her.

She looked at me, astonished. "Then we grew up together."

Nestled among the albums is the journal she kept that summer at Darien Lake. The entry for June 20:

Now I'm sitting on the grass, next to the water ski show and behind the Ferris wheel. There are gulls here—they remind me of home. So does the smell by the Ferris wheel—exactly like Market House chicken. It brings back a flood of memories of the City Dock in Annapolis. Dad and me at the Market House, regardless of the season or weather. Potatoes and chicken, wrapped in tinfoil...paper bags, napkins...walking arm in arm eating on the tiny ledge and staring out at the bleakness of the bay in winter. Only locals to look at—old men—fishermen, with caps, flannel shirts and jackets. Summer—chocolate ice cream from a sugar cone, dripping. Tourists in matching red, white and blue outfits. Colorful, preppy Annapolis. Main Street, the old bookshop, where Dad buys me three new books.

And walking on the rocks at the Naval Academy—extra fast—I'm good at this. Scan and step, scan and step quicker. The sea wall, wind whipping my hair back, feet on a slippery rock, waves splashing my feet. Extra splashes—the wake from the Harbor Queen. Wave to the tourists. They wave back, smiling. I wave to the boaters on the Severn River. Wish I were one of them. The Egg Harbor owners, with their Formica tables with dried flowers arranged in a vase; the living room of their vessel looks more like a house. Not salty at all! But look at this British racing green hull, a double-ender. There's a mahogany hull—two nut-brown sails, gaff-rigged, running, beautiful. Look at the upkeep on the wood. Wow! God, I miss those times.

A photo of Miriam, Myrna and Jackie, arm in arm, laughing. Miriam returned home from Darien Lake jubilant from her success and new friendships, especially with a young man named Jake. We had only three days to pack her for London. Only three days to be together.

Myrna and Tim spent her last evening with us. Myrna was seven months' pregnant with our first grandchild. As they were leaving for home, Miriam said, "Wait a minute."

She raced up the stairs and back down again. Cradling a three-foot-tall teddy bear, she held it out to Myrna. "I want you to have this," she said. Her sister reached out her arms for it. For many years the bear sat on Craig's bed, its fur flattened from two generations of hugs.

At ten o'clock that night, both of us totally worn out, Miriam and I finished the packing. She pulled a garment bag out of the closet.

"I haven't had a chance to model my new coat for you," she said. "Jake helped me pick it out in Buffalo." As she slid her arms into the sleeves, she was suddenly transformed into a brilliant burst of fire-engine red. She whirled around, striking a high-fashion runway pose.

"Jake told me I have beautiful legs," she said, laughing. She threw her arms around me and laid her head on my shoulder.

CHAPTER 8

Unexpected Gifts

HOW IS IT POSSIBLE FOR ANY PERSONAL BELONGINGS to survive an explosion at 31,000 feet—nearly six miles high? And even if they did, how could they survive intact, lying for days, even weeks, in the countryside exposed to the bitter Scottish winter? But they did. And because of the compassion and goodness of the people of Lockerbie, most of the Pan Am Flight 103 families got back at least a few of their loved one's belongings.

Lockerbie police and volunteers painstakingly combed an 845-square mile area and retrieved almost 18,000 items—clothes, cameras, film, wrapped holiday gifts, souvenirs, even whole suitcases. The Lockerbie police built a warehouse, where they inventoried and catalogued every item, even down to a single coat sleeve. They installed a washing machine and dryer. Volunteers washed and ironed every piece of clothing, every item in every mildewed suitcase, every pathetic scattered fragment. They carefully dried soggy diaries, letters, passports, wallets, school notebooks and term papers. They even ironed the pages of journals to keep them intact. Every item was returned to the families—carefully, lovingly wrapped in tissue paper, plastic bags and neat boxes. The Scottish police kept rolls of undeveloped film until they had finished their criminal investigation. They returned Miriam's film to me—in packages of developed large prints.

All these kindnesses and many more, the people of Lockerbie did and still do, for the families of those who died.

If Pam Am 103 had exploded just ten minutes later, it would have been over the Atlantic Ocean in such deep water that all would have been lost forever—the plane, the passengers, their personal effects. It also would have meant that any investigation of the cause of the explosion would have been impossible. I had no concept of the difficulties investigators would face in even a hundred feet of water until the explosion of TWA Flight 800 over Long Island Sound in July 1996.

A funny thing how, overnight, your priorities can shift. On the morning of December 21, my main worry was that Miriam would miss her connection to BWI and have to spend the night at JFK Airport. From the next day on, my deepest anxiety, my obsession, was to get her body returned home to us. Now Larry and I feel "fortunate" (how ironic to even use the word) that we were able to bury her in our family plot only eight miles from our home. Seventeen Pan Am families were not so lucky; their loved ones would never be recovered, just because of where they had the misfortune to sit in the plane.

My second obsession was to get her personal effects back—if there were any. The first week in February 1989, the Consulate General of the United States in Edinburgh sent me an affidavit to fill in and get notarized that I was the next of kin and legal guardian, entitled to receive Miriam's things. The Consulate General also asked me to send them a list describing everything Miriam had with her. Sure. This was something concrete I could do to help. I whipped out a yellow legal pad and pen. But the more I tried to recall everything she and I jammed into her suitcases, the more my memory fell short. And of course she bought many things overseas.

Help came from her friend Heather. Over a tearful supper at Bob's Big Boy in Annapolis, she described the textbooks they bought for their classes in London, the clothes Miriam wore, her jewelry. I gratefully wrote it all down on my pad. Then Heather dug deep into her purse and pulled out a blank book with a shiny gray cover.

"Miriam bought one of these to use as a journal," she said. "I liked it so much I decided to buy one for myself." I fingered its smoothness, turned it over and over and added it to my list.

Two months after Pan Am 103 exploded, I received the first of four packages of my child's personal belongings. My hands shook as I opened the tiny package. Inside I found one earring, a watch and only the metal loop from the other earring. Miriam was wearing them on the plane home. The silver earring was one of a pair she had received for Chanukah: tiny tragedy and comedy masks. My God! It was the lone tragedy mask that stared up at me from its plastic wrapper.

And the watch—a gift from my father on Miriam's twentieth birthday—it was still running!

On May 7, 1989, I received the second package, a huge box. I left work early to pick it up at the post office. It was so heavy the postmaster carried it to my car. He had a somber look on his face—he'd seen the return address.

I waited anxiously for Larry to get home from work. He carried the box from the car upstairs to Miriam's room—that was where I intended to open it. And I wanted him with me.

Inside the cardboard container sat my maroon soft-sided suitcase, the smaller of the two I had lent Miriam to take to London. It smelled musty and the frame was dented. But inside, meticulously wrapped, were her clothes: dresses, pants, socks, sweaters, swimsuit, tights and underwear, her shoes, her purses. Everything washed, ironed, folded neatly and wrapped in plastic bags. Many of the clothes were still in excellent, wearable condition. Surviving an explosion six miles high in the sky? Unfathomable.

I started crying and couldn't stop. As I lifted each item out, I remembered where we bought it and what she looked like wearing it. The red umbrella I bought only two days before she left for London to match her new red coat.

I discovered gifts. A fragile silver angel meant for the top of a Christmas tree. It was in almost perfect condition. A Frisbee from the Hard Rock Cafe in Amsterdam. A fat paperback of the British Museum filled with color photos. A navy blue Oxford University sweatshirt.

Delving deeper into the box, I discovered a packet of beautiful art cards on which Miriam had written holiday notes, not yet mailed. I'd mail them for her. Friends and relatives had already been informing me, reluctantly, afraid to upset me, that they'd received notes from Miriam a day or two after her death. At my request, they sent me copies or the notes themselves. Jim's mother and Miriam had corresponded from the time Miriam was seven. Grandma Bert sent me all seventy-five of her letters and cards.

Through my tears I saw a black book bag and another large carry-on, both crammed with books, notebooks and sheet music. They had crushed corners and a mildewed smell, but were all still readable.

And then I discovered Miriam's journal. I called it the Pooh Journal; a small lined notebook, the size and shape of an exam blue book. On the cover is an illustration of Winnie-the-Pooh and Piglet holding hands as they walk through the forest, with a caption: "It's so much friendlier with two."

Lying in the suitcase in the Scottish countryside, the journal, of course, got wet and muddy. The first ten pages were almost illegible. For the next two weeks, on my lunch hours at Westinghouse, I set the journal on an artist's light table as I deciphered the faded ten pages. The journal recorded her three-day trip to Wales with a friend. She wrote of the day, October 31, 1988:

This morning we got up early, showered, and Sheila, our friendly Welsh hostess, gave us breakfast. We found out that for £1.40 we could take a train to Kidwelly, a village with a castle from the year 1130. The train wasn't scheduled to leave till 12:30, so we set out on another walk—to a neighboring village that climbs a huge hill from which you can see for miles. We saw cats, an adorable huggable mutt, a stream, sheep on a hillside, fresh damp earth, leaves to crunch on as we stepped. At 11:30 Chris and I were back at the B&B collecting our things and being given a lovely little pamphlet by Sheila and her husband, Cyril.

The train ride took all of fifteen minutes! As we walked to the center of the village, a woman stopped her car next to me, asking where we were going and offered us a ride! Her name was Norma. We drove to the center of town and she stopped at a charming ice cream shoppe to ask about a B&B for us. Across the street was a B&B, run by two old women who tut-tutted around, preparing the beds for us. So Norma suggested we have a coffee at her home while the room was being prepared.

Thus began an amazing three-hour psychological orgy—talking about materialism, prejudice, Norma's life with her late husband and being accepted by his family; her children and her relationship with her daughter; priorities, death, grieving, learning.

"It's important to just go through life with your eyes open," Norma said. "People don't understand that there's a difference between 'Standard of Living' and 'Standard of Life.' As long as I can look out my window and see trees, I'll be happy."

We were thrilled, all three of us. Oh, what can happen when you open yourself up. You have to just leave yourself open to experiences—don't count anything out. We didn't and look at what happened to us.

"Today was so unique," Christine just said to me. And so it was. We saw the sun set from the beautiful church-yard cemetery across the street—the sun going down with the bare trees silhouetted against it, and Kidwelly Castle fitting neatly into the landscape. Smoke curling out of a new home's chimney—a new home right next to this Norman castle from the twelfth century. The church bells toll as I write this. Three horses galloping and staring at us from the field. The temperature, with the silent setting sun, dropped with the darkness. And hunger overtook us when we discovered the orientally decorated Queen Bee Restaurant. A wonderful meal served by yet more friendly Welsh people. The day can be summed up by this poem by Lu Yu, from *The Tao of Pooh:*

The clouds above us join and separate,
The breeze in the courtyard leaves and returns.
Life is like that so why not relax?
Who can stop us from celebrating?

THE THIRD BOX from Lockerbie arrived on my birthday, July 3, 1989. I lifted the cover off. There lay her address book: a history of her friendships over the past five years and now crammed full of all the new friends she'd made abroad. (I found it useful for years—she was helping me even then.) The box also contained the shiny gray book that Heather had admired; the second of Miriam's London journals. An excerpt:

10/1/88. I am sitting, as I always sit, on a grassy slope under a tree, surrounded by infinite shades of green and yellow. My shoes are off and I sit Indian style. People look at me as if I'm odd. It's the most touching and wonderful park scene I've ever seen. Two middle-aged, upper-middle-class fathers pushing their infants in strollers and talking. Old women alone on benches, dressed in their Sunday best. An elderly couple—the woman wearing a heavy coat though it's warm. Little dogs that yap, a playful golden retriever— every dog retrieving a ball. A squirrel scratching himself in the sunlight. Little boy with father—skipping with his blue balloon. Two little blonde girls with ponytails roller skating—they're both so graceful. Frisbee players, soccer players. An entire hill with people like me reading, meditating and writing . . . some on their stomachs, some on their backs, one with a Walkman and a notebook, one with sun-tan oil. Three soon-to-be delinquents on skateboards making too much noise, obstructing the natural balance. Three Indian boys—one on one bike, two on another—flying. A beautiful stylish man in a long gray coat that flows in the breeze as he walks swiftly away from me. A severe-looking woman in purple pants and a gray blazer buttoned to the neck with her tiny matching gray French poodle.

10/6/88. We're on the coach, on our way out of London, headed for the boat to Amsterdam. There's something about packing up and leaving anywhere that makes me introspective and a little sad. Despite the noncommittal drizzling, it's a beautiful evening. The sky is an icy pastel and tufts of clouds are vibrant in the sunset. Leaves are finally beginning to fall. Rush hour is about to erupt in full swing.

The Tao of Pooh is having a real effect on me. The whole idea that there's an overall plan for things and that the more we try to control and interrupt life's natural rhythm the farther we are from the truth. It's actually very important for me: the idea that over-intellectualizing leaves you with more unanswered (and often irrelevant) questions.

The idea that trying too hard is anti-productive—it goes against my grain, that line of thinking. I know that in certain instances, trying too hard does damage—an overly zealous mother can damage her children. But why is it such a crime to try too hard, to better myself, my relationships with people, my mind, my craft?

If I try to better myself and am passionate in that, I'm called a "perfectionist"—a supposedly unhealthy category. If I try too hard to better my mind, if I read and spell well as a result, then I'm an intellectual snob, trying to assert my self-congratulatory, superior attitude. (Is it being in theater that makes some of my classmates so anti-intellectual?) And, if I try too hard at my art, I get in my own way. I cease to be natural, released, free, spontaneous.

All children are ever taught is to "Try your best." But it ends up being detrimental. I don't know how to just exist—it doesn't feel like living. I'm tired of feeling guilty and inferior and stupid because I can't stop trying. What would they have me do? "People-pleasing"—it's turning into a dirty word.

But I have confidence in myself and I'm going to continue doing what I know is best for me. I need to keep reminding myself of what Isadora Duncan said in her book *And She Danced:* "Anyone can dance. Just put your hands to your heart and listen to your soul and you can dance. But most people are deaf."

DID I FEEL I was invading Miriam's privacy by reading her journals? No. They brought me closer to her. Going through her journals I felt a sense of amazement at the amount she had written, the outpouring of emotion and how much I was learning about her. Reading her journals was like having a conversation with her. The journals were as vivacious, as intellectual and as melodramatic as she was. She's alive in these pages, which are filled with little doodles, drawings and jokes, as well as reflections and quotes.

The Baltimore Sun and *The Capital* carried front-page stories about my receiving her journals from Lockerbie. The boxes contained all her London writings. Reading through them, I asked myself: What had I been missing? What might I find here in her own room? I began rummaging through her desk drawers. From her closet I pulled out cartons of her college and high school papers. I came upon a required journal that she kept for her "core" drama class at Syracuse. I found long-forgotten grade school papers, poems, wonderful art work, little diaries. Discovering her through these pages gave me enormous comfort. And distress. A diary entry when she was upset—she wasn't getting the attention she wanted from a boy she liked; it made me hurt, too.

In her closet I discovered Miriam the activist—a placard

she carried when she attended a pro-choice rally in Washington. On the back she wrote: "March 1987, my first protest march!"

In the musical *Mame*, there's a song "Open a New Window, Open a New Door." The boxes from Lockerbie introduced me to my daughter all over again. And sitting cross-legged on the rug in her room, I decided to write a book that would capture her spirit. Thus began what turned out to be my quest to immortalize my daughter.

In London she had bought no less than forty books. Many were textbooks and guidebooks, but other titles reflected a gigantic thirst for learning and a huge range of interests, especially in art, literature, drama and philosophy. *Love* by Leo Buscaglia, *A Critical Dictionary of Psychoanalysis*, *Guide to Yoga*, Shakespeare's sonnets. Miriam herself was something of a mystic and philosopher, a side of her I had not yet really begun to know.

I found no less than three copies of *The Tao of Pooh*, a book I'd never even heard of until she quoted it many times in her journals. Given that our favorite book to read together was *Winnie-the-Pooh*, I quickly opened it and learned what she meant about "life's natural rhythm" —how man so often disrupts the heavenly harmony of the universe. But suddenly I could read no more. I thought of the letter from her friend that Charles Kuralt read on *Sunday Morning*: "There is now a serious imbalance in the universe: Miriam Wolfe was aboard Pan Am Flight 103." It is not God's will that Miriam lies in a cemetery.

From that day on, her books became living, breathing things for me. Each time I look through the bookcases I discover something I don't remember ever seeing before. *Auto Repair for Dummies*, *The Two Sources of Morality and Religion*, *Postcards From the Edge*. When did those get there? I didn't see them yesterday and I go into her room almost every day—to wrap a gift, to get one of my dresses out of her closet. It's almost otherworldly.

She speaks to me through her books. There is *Zen and the Art of Motorcycle Maintenance*. Twenty years ago, I thought of it as a hippy book and my conservative side dismissed it. But now I tried again, searching for what Miriam might have seen in it. What I discovered was a profoundly moving story of a father and young son who had a difficult relationship and how their cross-country journey brought them in touch with nature, themselves and each other.

And *Act I* by Moss Hart—such an absorbing portrait of life in the theater. "Temperament is little else than a mask for panic," he writes, "and when people are panic-stricken, they of course behave badly. Why should they not?" I recalled all the hours, days even, before opening nights when Miriam stomped around the house— so irritable, so difficult and how exasperated she made me. She had stage fright, pure and simple. Well, not so simple. Understanding it might have ticked me off just as much.

The boxes from Lockerbie overflowed with art books. During one of her phone calls from London, she told me, "I just might get a Ph.D. in art history some day." Images of art often fill my mind when I think of my daughter. She was a swirl of Renoir pastels. Or a mosaic, a thousand rainbow facets melted into a vibrant reality. In high school, on the days I thought she'd never get to class on time, she was a Kandinsky, an abstract burst of frenzied colors rushing to catch the yellow school bus.

But now, in the blackest pigment of night, paintings crack and dissipate. Mary Cassatt's tender mother sits on the beach without her child. Renoir's mother in a blue dress now has no little hand to hold. In a Gainsborough family portrait, only a gaping emptiness remains where the daughter once stood.

At the bottom of the last box from Lockerbie, I found one of the last papers she wrote in London. I scanned it and thought, Oh, no, this is the bottom of the barrel—for me personally. I have a lot to learn about my daughter's attitude toward me. Maybe I don't need to know everything. Maybe I won't read it. But of course I did. Over and over. The paper discussed a play about a famed child psychoanalyst. But it was also about the two of us.

Mrs. Klein

The production of *Mrs. Klein* by Nicholas Wright at the National Theatre had a tremendous impact on me and forced me to seriously reanalyze many aspects of my life. Though psychoanalysis may be a remote subject for some, it is very much a part of my makeup. My grandfather, who is probably my biggest source of inspiration, is eighty-four years old and is a practicing psychoanalyst. His concern, like Melanie Klein's, is Freudian psychoanalysis. Not surprisingly, my grandfather's involvement in this aspect of medicine has had a profound effect on both my mother and me.

In the NT production, Melanie Klein destroys her relationship with her daughter, Melitta, because of an inability to stop acting as a psychoanalyst. Mrs. Klein has a cold, analytical approach to virtually every facet of her life, including her relationship with her children. This may seem imperceptible at first. But, once one is educated in psychiatric terminology, it's very easy to let Melanie Klein's problem get the best of you.

I identified very strongly with the character of Melitta. She is still struggling to find her identity—an identity separate from the one she knows with her mother. The fact that Melitta and Mrs. Klein are colleagues as well as mother and daughter complicates matters severely. Melitta was stripped of her self-worth as a child. She is also obsessed with winning her mother's approval, even though she knows intellectually that this is a futile effort. All of these factors contribute to making Melitta an extraordinarily complex and neurotic woman.

Naturally, my grandfather taught his children (my mother and her brother) the importance of self-awareness. This, in turn, has had a significant effect on my mother's relationship with me. My mother, in an attempt to instill in me a strong sense of self, raised me as an equal. This resulted in my struggle for an identity separate from my mother. For nine years, my mother and I lived alone together—and for obvious reasons are exceptionally close.

My grandfather's professional status has made me particularly aware of my motives for doing certain things. Recently, I have come to understand the psychological reasons for my constant search for mentors in older, more successful women. This search is a direct result of not having grown up worshipping my mother. I had respect for her, certainly. But because we were more like sisters than mother and daughter, I never went through the "normal" psychological process of thinking that my parents, particularly my mother, were perfect. So, I tried to transfer my stifled feelings onto other adult women whom I could emulate. *Mrs. Klein* actually had a great deal to do with this realization. *Mrs. Klein* also illustrates the frustration and unhappiness that sometimes accompany knowing a lot about one's own psychology. It becomes very difficult to act as a human being, without stopping to recognize, analyze and reanalyze the motivation behind the action.

AS I TUCKED *Mrs. Klein* back in the box, I grudgingly admired Miriam's intellect and at the same time wished I'd been the ideal mother. How come, so many years later, regrets and irritations still trespass into my head? One of her friends had the perfect mother. It wasn't so much her always-fastidious, appropriate clothes. It was that she never lost her temper; she was always patient and reasonable. (Yes, I was jealous, and apparently still am.) But the father of another of her friends once told me about his wife: "Never a cross word in thirty-two years." Good grief! Now that's over the top.

The exhilaration of climbing into my daughter's head through her writings had its flip side; it reinforced what I'd always known: that her sensitivity and insight produced a painful share of agonies and conflicts. The really tough part for me is the knowledge that there will be no more of her writings. But far worse is the knowledge that there's no more "us." Miriam was twenty when she died. I was twenty-one when my mother died. All three of us have been deprived of each other: the dialogues; the realness of arguments and exasperations; the struggle to understand one another and yet create our own sphere of independence; the comfort we would have given each other for years to come.

What I discovered is that comfort comes from unexpected places.

CHAPTER 9

Music to My Ears

STANDING ON OUR FRONT PORCH was an anxious-looking young woman, who handed me a long-stemmed pink rose.

"I just couldn't come before this," she said, her voice shaking. It had been eight months since Miriam died.

"That's all right," I replied, holding the door for her. "I knew you'd come eventually."

We sat in the living room and reminisced. She had arrived at Miriam's school in fourth grade, mature for her age—an exceptionally gifted musician and singer. With the predictable cruelty of kids, many classmates snubbed her for being different.

"I didn't think I'd be able to survive that year," she said. "Miriam made me feel I was worthy of being somebody's friend. When we sat together on top of the jungle gym and talked, I knew I was special." They remained friends over the years. Miriam spoke of her as "a musical genius."

We received nearly a thousand letters. I read and appreciated them all—some many times over. Of course, the expected condolences and kindnesses prevailed, but the numbers and distances staggered our imaginations. Before long, something more began to emerge, a theme repeated over and over: so many writing of a gift Miriam left with them. She affected their lives by way of encouragement, by way of understanding, by way of enlightenment. I thought I knew my daughter well, but I was discovering I hardly knew her at all.

At Bay Country Camp for the Theatre Arts, she forged friendships with other campers, the teachers and even Sharon Wyrrick, the camp coordinator. Miriam was only fourteen. It didn't matter to her that the staff members were adults; it was her philosophy that if she liked them, they would be her friends.

Sharon was also a well-known dancer and choreographer. In June 1989, the *Washington Post* carried this rave review: "Wyrrick is . . . one of the most gifted choreographers hereabouts. 'Storyboard for an Anxious Journey' [projects] a haunting and disquieting sense of mystery. We've seen it in her earlier works, but never more poignantly than in this work, which among other things is a dirge for a young friend who perished aboard the ill-fated Pan Am Flight 103."

Sharon dedicated the work to Miriam and told me: "Nothing I've ever done has been so well received. Miriam gave me a gift."

SENIOR YEAR, after Miriam finished a course in constitutional law, the teacher wrote her: "Your commitment to learning has been a huge factor in my maintaining some optimism about education. Please never abandon your convictions, integrity and capacity for greatness which make you so unique."

GRANDPA SAUL was her friend, mentor and role model, exuding humor and warmth, which made his constructive criticism palatable (and there was plenty of it). They had a private joke. When he called from his home in Milwaukee, he'd ask:

"So, Miriam, how are you doing in reform school?"

"Well, Grandpa, in my time off for good behavior, I'm doing a little acting, singing . . ."

One of his patients gave him the following quotation, framed; it sums up the way he lived his life and the way he taught Miriam to live hers:

"I expect to pass through life but once. If therefore there be any kindness I can show, or any good thing I can do to any fellow being, let me do it now and not defer or neglect it, as I shall not pass this way again."—William Penn.

She had been at Syracuse only a month when she called me, her voice filled with distress. "Mom, I have this friend who never eats. She keeps saying she just has to lose ten more pounds and then she'll feel better about herself. But I can tell she's starving herself. And in class today she fainted. She's anorexic, Mom. So after class I talked to the teacher." The responsive teacher immediately arranged for the friend to get counseling. Soon after, the self-destructive behavior stopped—and she did truly begin to feel better about herself.

This was not the first time Miriam tried to help a friend in trouble. I was collecting the carpool of fourteen-year-olds after a play audition in Annapolis. When I arrived at 9 p.m., I found only one kid standing on the sidewalk waiting. He told me one of the girls had started crying hysterically because she didn't get a part. She'd broken away from the group and run three blocks down the dark street. Miriam and her friends had run after her. As I pulled up to the curb, I saw them huddled around the sobbing girl, trying to comfort her. Her crying continued all the way to her house. I barely had time to put on the brake when Miriam, herself in tears, jumped out and ran straight into the kitchen.

"Something is very wrong," she blurted out to the girl's mother. "You have to do something. She's gone overboard." Several years later, the child attempted suicide—unsuccessfully, thank God. She's now happily married.

And another incident in high school: The younger sister of a friend whispered to her: "Everything's so lousy, I feel like jumping out a window." Miriam promptly alerted a guidance counselor, who set the wheels in motion for the girl to get into therapy.

OVER AND OVER I've heard a familiar chorus:. "Because of your daughter . . ." At a Colonial Players production in Annapolis: "It's because of Miriam that I'm here," an adult cast member told Larry and me. "She encouraged me to get back into acting. I had missed it so."

"Don't ever give up your music," she told my friend Donna. "You have such a beautiful voice." Donna got the lead in a local production of *Little Mary Sunshine* and choral singing is an essential part of her life today.

PROBABLY her most important activity in London was her formation of a new "alternative" theater group to bring back to the Syracuse drama department. With her close friend Theo Cohen and several other students, they sought to expand the department's traditional horizons. After Pan Am 103—and, by the way, Theo was also on the plane—the students who survived carried on and performed a play to introduce their new vision. One member of the group, Annie Lareau, explained in the program:

> The Add Libb Theatre Company is the product of a great desire to explore new theatrical venues and styles. . . . Theo and Miriam were the two brain children of the group. It was their hunger for political issues to be discussed through theater and brought to not only the department, but also the general public. They felt strongly that if theater was to survive it needed to reach fresh audiences. "Theater is not just for theater people," Miriam Wolfe said. The five of us set out to bring what we dreamed of being physical theater—mime, improvisation, playwriting seminars and guest speakers—to the department, to the campus at large and, ideally, to the more impoverished parts of Syracuse....

MIRIAM'S London roommate Jessica Genick, said, "She loved helping people. She also helped me decide what to do after graduation. I was at a loss."

"Try the Milwaukee Repertory Company, they have internships," Miriam suggested. "Use me as a reference." Miriam had been to Milwaukee in the spring of '88 to visit my father and they had taken a tour through the theater. She quickly developed a rapport with the director and sent her a postcard from London. Jessica spent several successful runs with the company.

Miriam wrote the following letter to her fifteen-year-old stepbrother, Chris Spencer, when she was a freshman at Syracuse. Three years older than Chris, she wanted to spare him some of the agonies of the college application process. Chris was accepted into and graduated from his first-choice college as an architecture major.

How to Apply to College: A Sister's Advice

The closer we get to Fall, the closer the college application process gets. And I remember what a frenzy I was in when I was going through the business of applying to schools. So, I decided to write you a letter that passes on all the stuff I learned from my experience. I hope it helps. OK, here we go. A Few General Points to Remember:

1. NOTHING IS WRITTEN IN STONE, which means that if you don't get into your first choice school, you can always apply as a transfer student after one year somewhere else. So, don't let any of this stuff overwhelm you. No matter what anyone tells you, this is not a life and death decision.

2. When looking at colleges, remember to consider more than just what you plan to major in. Make sure that if you choose a school for architecture it also will be a place where you can (a) play your trumpet, (b) play sports that are important to you, etc. Make sure you'll be able to do recreation type things that you enjoy.

3. Consider the size of the school (which, of course, affects classroom size), the location and the people. The people are probably the most important thing, because the people you go to college with really do have a big influence on your values and ideas for the rest of your life.

That's why it's important, if at all possible, to VIS-IT THE SCHOOLS YOU ARE CONSIDERING!! That way, you can decide what the school's really like. Please remember that the college brochures only tell their side of the story—they want to sell you on their school and they try to make you see it with rose-colored glasses. So, when you visit, ask if you can sit in on a class or two.

At my high school, seniors were allowed to visit colleges and it was considered an excused absence. You may want to find out if that's true at your school.

4. One of the things that makes the application process such a pain is that YOU HAVE TO TOOT YOUR OWN HORN! The thing that gets you into colleges is the thing they notice about you that is DIFFERENT from the other thousands of kids who apply. So, you have to emphasize the fact that you successfully completed two college-level architecture courses in your junior and senior years. Then, it won't matter as much if you don't have 1500 SAT scores. Seriously, Chris, that's the name of the game.

Emphasize your accomplishments, especially all the Band stuff. They like to see that kids can stick to something and do it well. Your accomplishments in that area will impress them.

OK, now let's talk about what to do in the early stages of applying to schools, which means September to December of your senior year.

1. Get recommendations from teachers and counselors done early. Why? Because they will get swamped with requests. Chances are, the teachers you choose to write recommendations for you are some of the best teachers in the school, which is why lots of kids'll be after 'em. The sooner they write your recommendation, the more specific they'll be about you and the more flattering their reports of you will be. After teachers write enough recommendations, they tend to get generic with their answers, which is the last thing you need. You want yours to sound different from the other 4,000 any college may receive.

2. Most schools give their applicants the option of having an interview. Interviews work in one of two ways: you either interview at the school itself, or you do an "alumni" interview (an interview in your home town with a graduate of the school). Generally, interviews at the school itself carry more weight than alum ones, because they're conducted by the actual staff . . .the Dean of Admissions, etc. (But alum interviews are better than nothing.)

Why are interviews important?? Because they show that you (a) are a person with direction, (b) are articulate, (c) are a genuine, honest, sweet guy. They can't hurt—it's important to stress your individuality, so, unless the idea of an interview situation really bothers you, I'd give it a whirl.

3. Lastly, it's really important to make every college think that it is your first choice. What I mean by this is, take care with every application. Don't let on, from the way your application looks, that you've taken any less care than if it were another school.

DON'T FORGET to apply to some safety schools (schools you know you'll get into). You want to make sure you give yourself as many options as possible.

Most of all, Chris, please try to remember that everything happens for a reason. Everything will work out for the best. Just do the best you can and be gentle with yourself. Please don't hesitate to call me if you have a question, or just need to talk. I remember this whole scene very clearly.

No matter what, do what's best for you. Your parents will still love you. And, of course, so will I. I'm sooo proud of you. I also miss you a great deal. So, dear brother, I'll sign off. With All My Love, Miriam.

The *Washington Post* published her letter in Style Plus on December 4, 1992. It touched off a wave of letters from kids, parents and teachers telling us how valuable her advice had been. High school guidance counselors posted it on their bulletin boards. And on April 27, 1997, the letter was published again in a special college section in the *New York Daily News*.

It has been said that a grain of poetry suffices to season a century. More than two decades after she wrote it, Miriam's letter is nurturing another generation.

CHAPTER 10

"Thanks for Everything"

By Jake Stigers

I MET MIRIAM WOLFE in June of 1988. We had summer jobs performing in shows at Darien Lake, an amusement park near Buffalo, New York. My show was a Broadway revue and hers was a pop show, comprising popular music from the last four decades.

We discovered each other right away in rehearsals and became close friends almost instantly. Alone in a strange new city, Miriam and I were relieved to find at least one genuine friend with whom to spend the summer. We were also excited to find, in each other, a friend who shared the same cultural and intellectual interests.

We didn't agree on everything, though. She was an ardent feminist and much to her chagrin, I had only a passing interest in the feminist cause. We often had heated disagreements over the relative importance of many works of literature or current events. The two of us also didn't see eye-to-eye regarding Dustin Hoffman's ability as an actor. She thought he was talented. Before I met Miriam, I considered any disagreement between friends a manifestation of personal hatred. I could not be friends with someone with whom I did not share almost the same opinions and values. Needless to say, I had few true, close friends. Miriam showed me that friends can disagree and that often an argument can lead to an education or a strengthening of a relationship.

Miriam exposed me to a lot that summer. She introduced me to the joys of discussing literature and musical theater over baked brie and white zinfandel. She whiled away most of her free time between her shows plowing through Ayn Rand's *The Fountainhead*, a weighty tome that only began to whet her insatiable appetite for mental stimulation. Miriam couldn't believe I had never, as an English major, heard of Rainer Maria Rilke's *Letters to a Young Poet* and she gave me her very own copy to make sure I would have this book in my personal library.

When summer finally ended, I assumed we would remain faithful pen pals at best and maybe not see each other for at least a few years, as is normally the case with the friends one makes while working in theme park shows around the country.

After the fall semester was well under way, I was delighted to get an overseas call one afternoon from her. She missed me and just wanted to hear my voice. We chatted for a few expensive, precious minutes and joked that it would be great if I could somehow visit her in London. I must have later mentioned that conversation to my mom, because a few days later, completely out of character, she told me that I "only live once" and I should go to visit Miriam. I quickly ordered a passport and called Miriam to tell her she was to have company.

I arrived in London's Gatwick Airport at 9 a.m. after a freezing and sleepless flight over the Atlantic. From somewhere to my right, I heard a cheerful salutation, "Jake, my dear! How are you?" I turned my head and instantly saw Miriam. She was practically doing handsprings to get my attention.

Let me digress a second here. You know those toy dolls with the strings you pull that make their arms and legs flail spastically? Imagine one of those dolls with the trademark buoyant Muppet walk and a head of big, bouncy curls that accent each exuberant body movement. Now add a sophisticated Barbra Streisand nose, a perpetually cheery grin with a slight head tilt and a practical-yet-classic (size six) wardrobe from, say, The Gap. That's Miriam.

We ran to see each other and hugged for what seemed to

be twenty minutes. After we realized we were in the way of the other passengers, we walked to the in-airport train station arm-in-arm, talking all the time. At the tube station we waited in line, still gossiping and giggling, so I could buy a week-long tube pass. The man in front of us got into a fight with the ticket seller over some discrepancy in change and shouted in a genuine cockney accent, "Piss off!" Miriam turned to me with the biggest grin on her face and said in her best cockney, "Welcome to London!" Our gales of laughter no doubt betrayed the fact that we were genuine tourists.

Thus began my fast-paced, incredible week in London. The first place Miriam took me that morning, after we had dumped my stuff at her Kensington Park flat, was the Museum of the Moving Image, a fascinating exhibit of the history of filmmaking. Halfway through the museum I suddenly felt a rush of uncontrollable exhaustion. Yup. Jet lag. Miriam somehow steered me back to her flat for a long nap. We tried again the next day, after having spent a leisurely afternoon in the flat and having eaten a tasteless dinner at a trendy European vegetarian restaurant.

Before the week was over, we had spent significant amounts of time in four art museums, including the Wallace Collection, an obscure little private gallery where Jean-Honoré Fragonard's *The Swing* hangs. Miriam and I shared a mutual passion for Rococo art and *The Swing* was one of our favorite works. She just happened to know it was housed at this quaint little museum. Once we were finally standing together before our painting, displayed in an exquisite Victorian setting, our perpetual giggling stopped and all we could do was stand in awe and allow the passionate swirls of color emanating from the canvas to bathe us in their intricate, breathtaking beauty. We had to come back to gaze at it four more times before we decided to leave the museum. Before we left, though, we each bought expensive prints of the work in the museum gift shop and I was elected to carry them carefully for the next eight hours of sightseeing in downtown London.

Miriam and I also took in three shows that week (including *Les Miserables* and Stephen Sondheim's *Follies*) and attended mass in an awe-inspiring cathedral (though her family is Jewish and mine is Protestant). We even had lunch in an authentic pub and made Thanksgiving dinner with some of her friends from school in their flat—in the same building where (then) internationally famous pop singer George Michael lived.

Miriam and I both loved language and grammar and we were perpetually amused by the odd constructions and foreign trends in European advertising as we read the posters on the Tube. Our favorite joke concerned the tear-jerking narratives of convicted "fare fiddlers," people who try to ride without paying.

We spent one of my last nights in London in an enormous old bookstore. As we explored the tall dark aisles of shelving, I came across a book that had changed my ways of thinking: John Berger's *Ways of Seeing*, a fascinating collection of essays on perception and subliminalism in society. I brought the book to Miriam's attention, expecting her already to have read and dissected it in countless literature and art classes. To my complete shock, she hadn't. I made her buy it and promise to read it before she reached the States in December. A few aisles later, we encountered Sally Swain's *Great Housewives of Art*, a feminist repainting of Western art from the last three centuries. Since the book doubled us over in laughter, we each bought a copy.

My too-short visit in London over, Miriam and I exchanged tearful farewells and promised to write as soon as we could. The last time I saw her she was standing on a little boulevard in the street. Her roommates had given us a terrible time about the fact that we both owned black penny loafers, so we made sure we always wore them together. She was grinning and jumping around and waving to me as my taxi whisked me to the Tube station that would take me to Heathrow Airport. We wrote each other quite a lot and called with even more frequency than before, our recent reunion reminding us of the fact that we missed each other so much.

On the morning of December 21, my semester finals all safely behind me, my dad picked me up at school to take me home for Christmas vacation. As we pulled into the driveway, my mother appeared beside the car, crying and shaking uncontrollably. Through her sobs she told us: Miriam's plane went down.

We walked slowly into the house. I told myself that I didn't know anything for sure, so I refused to get emotional. My Dad turned on CNN and my family stared in numb helplessness at television footage of the plane wreckage strewn about Lockerbie, Scotland.

Life went on the next eight months. Accepting Miriam's death wasn't impossibly difficult for me because, all alone in Iowa, I certainly wasn't used to seeing her all the time so I didn't suddenly have a void in my life in her absence. I miss her most whenever some reminder of one of our countless inside jokes comes to my attention and I realize I really can't call her any more to share in my laughter.

Sunday, September 10, 1989, I finally made it to Severna Park to visit Miriam's family. Her mother and I went through some of Miriam's things that had been recovered from the 845-square-mile crash site. I was shocked to find *Ways of Seeing* and *Great Housewives of Art* among those recovered items. They were water-logged and covered with Scottish dirt, but they had survived the crash.

We went to the cemetery so I could have an official good-bye. The rectangle of half-dead sod that covered her new grave seemed to me to be a morbid joke. How could Miriam's body, perpetually in a state of exuberant motion, be dead and buried? There seemed no possible way that that brown turf and that gravestone could hold her still.

It is an uncomfortable feeling to lose a friend in an international tragedy. I can be driven to an overwhelming state of grief whenever a story about the bombing appears on the news. Miriam had had a dramatic and commanding presence while she lived. Hers was a full, rich life and she certainly made a mark on many other lives. Perhaps the only way for a visible, essential person such as Miriam to go would be in a way that the whole world would know about it. Her final curtain call had international coverage and will be recalled for years to come when other planes are brought down by terrorists' bombs.

Thanks for everything, Miriam. I miss you.

JAKE STIGERS is now an advertising copywriter and creative director in Chicago. His essay "Surviving the Bombing of Pan Am Flight 103: The Loss of Innocence and a Dear Friend in an International Tragedy" was published in the January-March 1998 issue of the scholarly *Journal of Personal & Interpersonal Loss.*

Love and Anguish

The *Honolulu Advertiser* gave *Miriam's Gift* a full-page review on February 26, 2000. The reviewer wanted more details about the inner Miriam: "It's not clear, for example, whether or not she was in love with the young man who visited her in England. This is not merely nosiness; the reader grows to appreciate Miriam's joie de vivre and her exceptional caring so much that you can't help but wish her this gift—to have fallen in love—before her untimely death."

Here's the answer. Miriam fell in love with Jake Stigers, heart and soul. Her love proved both exhilarating and a source of deep anguish. During their summer at Darien Lake she wrote this poem:

Inertia

A speeding train
Waylaid by a cruel conductor
And detoured onto not-yet-laid tracks.
Brake.
Are those sparks?
Now? Stoppp.
Snap.
My neck
Shock
Numbing.

She handed it to me to read during the week I visited her at Darien Lake. I shook my head, confused. I had no idea what it meant— until she explained. Jake, a handsome, talented, loving man, is gay.

She wrote a second poem in London called "He Is Gone." I found it among her writings sent to me by the Scottish police. It was an intensely private poem, in which she combined lyrics of mostly unhappy love songs from several Broadway musicals. Reading it over and over, I felt ashamed that I hadn't understood, or at least intuited, these moments of despair.

CHAPTER 11

From Mourning to Lobbying

ON JANUARY 18, 1989, THE BITTER COLD EXPRESSED our collective mood. We were gathered together at a Syracuse Sheraton, the families of the thirty-five Syracuse University students killed aboard Pan Am 103. Most of us were meeting each other for the first time, together in sorrow and for solace, for the university service to memorialize our children. For the first time, we did not feel alone.

More than 10,000 students and faculty attended the solemn service in the Carrier Dome, which concluded with an impassioned goodbye to each of our children. At Hendricks Chapel thirty-five memorial books, each one bearing the student's name in gold, were set out on tables lit by candles. Friends, faculty and parents stood in long lines to write their thoughts and farewells.

The same night, seven families attended a special drama department memorial service. For three hours, drama students and faculty moved us to emotions we never thought possible with original songs, dances, poems and memories. Through our tears we were startled to find ourselves even laughing about our kids' quirks and escapades. One of Miriam's friends from home reminisced about "the Maryland Miriam."

"Mir loved the piano bar we used to frequent at a pub called Marmaduke's. It was always our first date when we got back from SU. She loved to get up and sing 'Cockeyed Optimist' from *South*

Pacific or 'Don't Cry for Me, Argentina' from *Evita*. She always sang beautifully, but it didn't matter—she would always come back to the table, sit down and brood about every mistake she had made in the song."

I broke into helpless laughter.

WHEN Pan Am 103 exploded over foreign soil, there were 183 Americans on board. We had every reason to believe our State Department had procedures in place for handling an international catastrophe like ours with speed and sensitivity. Right? Wrong. The State Department had no system for notifying next of kin—not even for obtaining a copy of the airline manifest. On December 21, that blackest of days, Pan Am didn't call us and neither did the State Department. Weeks later, when identified bodies were finally shipped home, the families awaiting their loved ones' remains at JFK found themselves in a degrading situation. The bodies had been transported like cattle to a cargo area of the airport. We personally were spared that humiliation.

The families who congregated in the Syracuse Sheraton were politically motivated. Outraged at our government's inaction and insensitivity, intensely angered by Pan Am's behavior, we united to form the Victims of Pan Am Flight 103 (VPAF103). VPAF103 would become a powerful, effective lobbying group.

Labeling ourselves "victims" was not an arbitrary decision. The Justice Department defines a victim as a person who has suffered direct or threatened physical, emotional or monetary harm as a result of the commission of a crime. In the case of a victim who is deceased, the following are also considered victims: a spouse, a parent, a legal guardian, a child, a sibling, another family member or any person designated by the court.

Our new group asked the State Department to return the remains not yet received, as well as personal effects, in an expeditious, humane manner. We were determined to secure victims' rights and to correct flaws in the system that led to insensitive, abusive treatment of the surviving families. We also planned to serve as a victims' support group and source of information to the families.

We called for a government investigation to determine all those responsible for such a horrendous crime and how it was carried out. We also demanded a separate concurrent government investigation into how an informed government and a prestigious, worldwide American-based carrier permitted this tragedy to occur. Could it have been avoided? Were there mistakes, wrongful procedures and negligence that created the climate for such a crime? We wanted to ensure that a Pan Am 103 would never happen again. At this first meeting on January 18, Larry and I distributed copies of the op-ed piece we published in the *Baltimore Sun* just twelve days earlier. Larry wrote it; I edited it.

Six Proposals on Airplane Terrorism

With the loss of our beloved Miriam, we present six suggestions to help prevent future acts of terrorism.

(1) This plea we direct at the media: Articles that give public recognition to individual terrorists and the groups or ideals they serve further the terrorist's purpose—as a child smashes a toy in order to obtain parental attention. We suggest that the phrase "an identified terrorist or fanatical group has claimed credit" be substituted for any actual known names . . .

(2) We propose an international agreement among manufacturers to provide plastic explosives with an odor additive within the sensory range of specially trained dogs and a trace of radioactive ingredient within the sensory range of ordinary detection instruments. These additives would go a long way toward the prevention of transportation bombings.

(3) The luggage compartments of aircraft could be isolated by a blast-proof shield and vented outward for the expanding gases normally associated with an explosion.

The compartment itself could be jettisoned to restore fly-ability and control.

(4) Once luggage is inspected, each piece should be marked with a large paper stick-on band that would encompass the entire article. A numbered passenger along with numbered luggage would make last-minute switching more difficult.

Carry-on luggage should be further limited in size and similarly numbered. In the cabin, closed-circuit TV cameras wired to blast-protected (in-flight) recorders might reveal strange activity preceding an act of on-board terrorism and lead to insight for future adjustments. This scheme apparently works in the banking system.

(5) From mid-afternoon on that fateful Wednesday until after midnight we were unable to determine whether our Miriam was actually on board. Friends, relatives and the media occupied the phone lines and turned that evening into a nightmare of re-dialings. We believe a standing task force—of the U.S. State Department for international flights and the FAA for domestic flights—should step in immediately and establish channels to the next-of-kin without fear of legal repercussions or incurring liability.

(6) Lastly, let there be an agency whose sole purpose is to solicit and examine ideas from just plain people. It is too late to prevent the death of our dear Miriam, but if one life can be saved by one of our thoughts, the fact that she inspired it will give proof that she lived and will continue to live in our hearts.

MARYLAND Senator Barbara Mikulski entered our op-ed into the *Congressional Record* and sent copies to William Sessions, then director of the FBI, and to Rep. Dante Fascell, chairman of the House Committee on Foreign Relations. Rep. Sessions forwarded a copy to the head of the FAA. Rep. Fascell wrote to thank us.

President Ronald Reagan had one more month in office when Pan Am 103 exploded. Yet he issued not one word of condolence to the families, either public or private. (An ugly rumor surfaced that President Reagan and Prime Minister Margaret Thatcher spoke on the phone and decided to downplay the disaster. The rumor was never confirmed.)

On April 3, 1989, VPAF103 gathered at Lafayette Park directly across the road from the White House. We heaped flowers on a temporary shrine and stated our purpose: to protest our government's lack of action. President George Herbert Walker Bush was now in office. He too was silent.

It was at Lafayette Park that my friendship began with Peggy and Ann, Maryland residents whose daughters were among the Syracuse students on the plane. VPAF103, feeling empowered, established a newsletter. Many families actively spoke out and began to haunt the halls of Congress.

Belatedly, on April 6, in direct response to the families' protests, President Bush sent a condolence letter to each family, vowing to "identify the cowardly murderers" and improve airport security. Responding to the unyielding commitment of the families, he issued, on August 4, 1989, an Executive Order forming the seven-member President's Commission on Aviation Security and Terrorism. Ann McLaughlin, former U.S. Secretary of Labor, chaired the commission, which also included two senators, two congressmen, a former Secretary of the Navy and a just-retired Air Force general. The commission conducted a thorough six-month review of existing security, options for handling terrorist threats and the treatment of victims.

On May 15, 1990, the families were ushered through the security checkpoint into the imposing Executive Office Building. We had been invited to a State Department briefing of the commission's findings. President Bush spoke briefly, questions were answered and each family received a copy of the report and an American flag. The flags were given in the same spirit as those given to military dead—because a crime had been committed against the United States, not merely against individuals. A hushed, heavy atmosphere prevailed. Some of us had lost whole families. A grandfather accepted four flags in memory of his son, daughter-in-law and two young grandchildren.

The commission's most devastating finding confirmed what we already knew and would have to live with for the rest of our lives: this tragedy need never have happened. Highlights of the commission's blunt and well-documented report:

The U.S. civil aviation security system is seriously flawed and has failed to provide the proper level of protection to the traveling public. The FAA is "far too reactive to problems instead of anticipating them" and pays far too little attention "to human factors and training." Pan Am's security lapses and the FAA's failure to enforce its own regulations followed a pattern that existed for months prior to Flight 103, on the actual day of the tragedy and—notably—for nine months thereafter.

The report is filled with "shoulds."

Congress should create the position of Assistant Secretary of Transportation for Security and Intelligence, an appointment with tenure to establish a measure of independence. Using FAA resources, the federal government should manage security at domestic airports through a system of federal security managers.

The United States should pursue a more vigorous counterterrorism policy. The State Department should conduct negotiations with foreign governments to permit U.S. carriers operating there to carry out FAA-required screening and other security precautions.

In addition, the FAA should launch a top priority R&D program to produce technology that will detect small amounts of plastic explosives at airports. Does the public have a right to be notified of threats to civil aviation? Yes, the report says, under certain circumstances. Victims of terrorist actions against the U.S. Government should qualify for special financial compensation. And the victims themselves must be given higher priority. The State Department must ensure that families of victims receive prompt, humane and courteous treatment and service in overseas disasters.

DESPITE our rising power as a lobbying group and the gratifying response of the President's Commission, some family members' philosophies and personalities clashed. A number of families split into a second group, Victims of Pan Am 103/Lockerbie. Miriam's stepmother and others headed it. Larry and I continued to support both groups. But it wasn't long before I opened my *Washington Post* one morning and discovered a mean-spirited story about the split. I published a rebuttal on the *Post's* "Free for All" page.

My point was that dissension eventually afflicts many organized groups of survivors because they are diverse human beings brought together solely by tragic events. But gossiping about the group conflicts took attention away from our hard work to get the current legislation through Congress—a bill that would improve airline security and might even prevent another Pan Am 103. I also appealed to the *Post* to start attacking the Bush administration for its absolutely inexcusable rapprochement with Iran and Syria. Both were—and still are—on the State Department's list of countries that foster terrorism.

Despite the families' differences, our goals coincided and almost two years of painstaking lobbying paid off. Congress enacted the Federal Aviation Security Improvement Act of 1990. President George Herbert Walker Bush signed it into law on November 6. Senator Frank Lautenberg praised the families: "They've been tireless in their efforts to try to make sure that others are spared their grief. This legislation is a testament to their efforts and dedication."

Basically, the new law called for speeding up development

of technologies to detect explosives. Training standards for security personnel were to be upgraded and federal aviation security managers were to be appointed within two years at all major airports—to replace private contractors now handling the job.

The new law also covered foreign air carriers. Those flying to and from the United States had to comply with the same security measures required of U.S. carriers. Warning provisions were to be strengthened. Better guidelines were to be established for notifying flight and cabin crews of a security threat. Better procedures were to be developed to notify passengers of credible terrorist threats.

The secretary of state was also directed to publicize rewards offered for information leading to the arrest of terrorists. And the State Department was required to improve its procedures for dealing with the families of terrorist victims.

In the flush of triumph over the bill's passage, the VPAF103 newsletter reminded us of Hubert Humphrey's words: "Life's unfairness is not irrevocable. We can help balance the scales for others, if not always for ourselves."

THE MOST agonizing question remained unanswered: Who committed this crime? From the very day of the explosion, the U.S. Government had marshaled the departments of State and Justice, the FBI and the CIA and combined forces with the Scottish police and Scotland Yard to hunt down those responsible for the bombing.

Two months prior to the downing of Pan Am 103, in October 1988, West German authorities raided a number of Frankfurt area residences where members of the Popular Front for the Liberation of Palestine-General Command (PFLP-GC) were reportedly holed up in "safe houses." Sixteen were arrested. Police discovered Toshiba radio-cassette recorders that had been tampered with—each one rigged as a bomb with a barometric trigger device, the kind of device used in previous attacks on civilian aircraft.

Inexplicably, by the end of October, all but three of the

Palestinians had been released by the German courts. Intelligence sources determined that six bombs had been made. The German authorities found five. One was still missing. Eventually, it seems to have been transported to the Mediterranean island of Malta, where it was packed in a bronze-colored Samsonite suitcase, along with clothing purchased in Malta. The suitcase was placed aboard a Malta-to-Frankfurt flight. In Frankfurt, the unaccompanied inter-airline luggage was transferred to Pan Am 103, a Boeing 727, for the European leg of the flight. I don't know why the bomb didn't explode on the flights from Malta and Frankfurt. Perhaps the crucial altitude criterion had not been met on those flight legs. The plane would later be traveling at a far higher altitude over the Atlantic. In London at Heathrow Airport, the luggage was transferred to a Boeing 747, the *Clipper Maid of the Seas*, for Pan Am Flight 103's transoceanic flight bound for New York and Detroit.

The *Clipper Maid of the Seas* took off, headed north over England and crossed the Scottish border. Thirty-seven minutes later, it blew up.

In 1991, after two years of worldwide investigation, the United States indicted two Libyan intelligence agents, Lamen Khalifa Fhimah and Abdel Basset Ali Megrahi. They were, respectively, the station chief and former security chief of Libyan Arab Airlines in Malta. It was believed that Megrahi was the senior officer in the Libyan intelligence service and director of its Center for Strategic Studies in Tripoli.

The brilliant investigative skills of the Americans, British and Scottish cannot be emphasized too strongly. Combing almost a thousand square miles of Scottish countryside for clues, they found two significant fragments—each smaller than a fingernail. One turned out to be a piece of circuit board from a Swiss timing device that was sold to a high-level Libyan intelligence official; the other was a piece of the Toshiba radio-cassette circuit board. Investigators also found tiny bits of clothing that they traced to a shop in Malta—clothing that wound up stuffed into the Samsonite suitcase carrying the bomb.

Fhimah and Megrahi served only as the final means to an end. This was an act of state-sponsored sabotage. It was widely believed that three governments conspired in the bombing. Iran paid for it in seeking revenge for the accidental shooting down of an Iranian Airbus by the U.S. Navy missile cruiser *Vincennes.* Syria trained the terrorists. And the Libyan government carried out the act.

When nations officially foster mass murder, can there be any expectation of justice?

From the very day Miriam's plane exploded, Pan American World Airways chose to take the adversarial role. Liability, not compassion, was their primary concern. Shortly after Miriam's death, we received two ominous letters. One arrived from the Chairman of the Board of Pan Am, defensively protesting the airline's innocence of wrongdoing. The second letter came from Pan Am's insurance carrier, U.S. Aviation Underwriters, offering to settle the case. If we accepted their offer, we would absolve Pan Am of any wrongdoing.

Larry and I met with Miriam's father and stepmother and immediately agreed not to accept the offer. First of all, Miriam's life was priceless. Having to articulate it in terms of monetary worth sent shivers up my spine. And we all agreed that if we accepted the money we would be sending the message to Pan Am that it was blameless. The four of us fervently believed that Pan Am did not provide the security it had promised its passengers.

Early in 1989, Miriam's father and I joined a lawsuit against Pan Am, charging the airline with willful misconduct, fraud and negligence in its security procedures. In pursuing the suit, the law firm representing us, Kreindler & Kreindler, sent me fifty-six "interrogatories"—categories of personal questions I was to answer about Miriam: Her entire history: schools, grades, teachers; her salaries and supervisors of all her jobs; her illnesses, doctors, dentists, orthodontist, everything. What an ordeal.

But these legal questions and answers didn't tell who Miriam really was, so I wrote a ten-page essay about her, "Miriam Luby

Wolfe, My Daughter, My Friend" and sent it with the interrogatories. And with this essay I began a book about Miriam and our life together. It was the beginning of my years-long quest to immortalize my daughter.

Thus began three years of obstruction and delaying tactics by Pan Am, as well as severe restrictions imposed on the victims by the presiding judge. But the victims prevailed. On July 10, 1992, a jury in U.S District Court found Pan Am guilty of willful misconduct. Highlights of the findings:

- Pan Am did not comply with FAA regulations, which required that unaccompanied inter-airline luggage be hand-searched, not just X-rayed. Nor was the pilot informed that an unaccompanied bag was on board.
- Because the airline was in financial trouble, it cut corners, severely limiting its security measures. Pan Am employed undertrained or completely untrained personnel and provided only minimal training. In Frankfurt, training materials, videos and booklets were often in English—a language often not understood by the airline's X-ray operators and security inspection personnel stationed at the security check station.
- Pan Am managers failed to disseminate U.S. State Department warnings of bomb threats to employees who could act upon them. The State Department's Toshiba Report warned of the existence of tampered cassette players housing plastic explosives and triggering devices. The report noted that German authorities had raided terrorist safe houses and found such devices. They provided descriptions and model numbers. A simple search of the only unaccompanied bag destined for Flight 103 would have uncovered the cassette bomb.
- The U.S. Embassy in Helsinki received a call that a Pan Am flight from Frankfurt to the United States would be destroyed between December 5 and 19, 1988. At least some

Pan Am security personnel in Frankfurt knew about it. The report was buried in other paperwork at Pan Am's Frankfurt station and later postdated to give the appearance that it had been received after Pan Am 103 was bombed.

• Pan Am engaged in widespread fraudulent security tactics, such as charging each passenger an extra $10 for "additional security," trumpeting this bonus feature in full-page newspaper ads. The truth? The extra fee went into the airline's general revenue fund and never found its way into improved security measures.

• Pan Am also claimed it had dogs specially trained to detect explosives at JFK Airport. Company executives appeared in television commercials with these dogs. The truth? The animals were ordinary curs rented for the day from a Long Island kennel.

THREE MORE years of delays and obstructions would follow before Pan Am settled with the individual families. Vindication has been bittersweet. Historically, executive suite villains get off scot-free. It is common knowledge that the main reason a business incorporates is to limit shareholders' liability to the value of the shares they hold. This, of course, is a necessary consideration for a business in raising entrepreneurial capital; if shareholder liability were not limited, nobody would buy stock. Corporate directors elected by the shareholders enjoy the same limited liabilities. When a corporation engages in the legal business activities prescribed by its prospectus, this limited liability is fitting and proper.

I believe that when a corporation is found guilty by a court of law of a willful crime, then the protection of the corporate umbrella should not be available to the directors. The corporate entity has no will of its own. It has, instead, corporate policy and corporate will implemented consciously by its directors. In this case, Pan Am's policies encouraged employees to neglect their responsibilities and, far worse, these policies led to death and destruction. Why, then, aren't the directors and hands-on managers of a guilty corporate entity held criminally accountable?

A group of directors and executives brought dishonor and destruction to a prominent pioneer in the airline industry. Pan Am went out of business.

When TWA Flight 800 exploded in July 1996, I ached for the families. Again, interminable delays. TWA personnel stalled in turning over the manifest and obstructed efforts of New York City officials to help the victims' families. On the plus side, only one week after the explosion, the U.S. Department of Justice and the U.S. Attorney's Office distributed a useful and compassionate booklet to the victims containing "Information and Assistance for Surviving Family Members."

The U.S. Government is now taking a tougher stand against terrorists. I wish the media would too. It has always grieved me to see vast TV coverage and front-page stories on Timothy McVeigh, the convicted murderer of 168 innocents in Oklahoma City; the sympathetic pieces on the Unabomber; profiles of Palestinian terrorists; and the two Libyan bombers. Not to mention the coverage, after September 11, 2001, of Al Qaeda's leader, Osama bin Laden. Our media lionize criminals, who must surely conclude: See how much publicity they give us? They really take us seriously.

Airlines at only two U.S. airports in mid-1997 had high-tech equipment in place to detect chemical explosives. In 1996 there were twenty-one other such detectors in use around the world. Our victims' newsletter, *Truth Quest*, asked: "Why does Manchester, England, have more state-of-the-art detectors than the entire United States?"

Our government is testing new technology in the building of airplanes: reinforced cargo holds to withstand the impact of an explosion. But don't look for airplanes containing such logical improvements any time soon.

For our own safety, major U.S. airports now impose a vast range of security measures. As annoying as the elaborate screening procedures can be, I consider them necessary. Unattended bags are confiscated. Each airline has a "No-fly" list. Many of the regulations have been triggered by passengers attempting to carry bombs or bomb-making chemicals aboard.

Late in 1996, President Clinton signed the Terrorism Prevention Act into law. Among other provisions, it amended the Foreign Sovereign Immunities Act to allow U.S. citizens to sue governments that sponsor terrorism. As a result, many Pan Am families filed a civil suit against Libya. In lobbying for the new law, Pan Am 103 families joined forces with other victims, including families of the Oklahoma City bombing, the first World Trade Center bombing, the Korean Airlines 007 disaster and the daughters of Leon Klinghoffer, whom terrorists murdered in 1985 aboard the cruise ship *Achille Lauro*.

In 1991 the United Nations imposed economic sanctions against Libya to force the handing over of the accused Fhimah and Megrahi, but to no avail. A group of U.S. senators and representatives, including Sen. Ted Kennedy, urged tougher sanctions—an oil embargo against Libya—but the UN would not agree to it. Too many countries were buying Libyan oil.

CHAPTER 12

Grief and Healing

"GRANDMA? We sang 'You Are My Sunshine' in school today and I want you to sing it with me," seven-year-old Leah said. "But Mom told me it makes you cry."

I couldn't answer her. I was fixing supper in our Honolulu apartment and suddenly I was transported to my Severna Park kitchen. Miriam and I were doing dishes together and singing "You Are My Sunshine," harmonizing joyously as we so often did on so many songs. How I ache for those moments. My voice was strong then, but I hardly ever sing any more. The notes now come out ragged and my range has shrunk from disuse.

Leah's sister, Alena, tiptoed into the kitchen, and in her small, sweet voice she said, "We're your sunshine now."

I gathered them both in my arms. We sang.

When Miriam died, Craig and Alena were newborns, Ben and Leah would arrive two years after, and Emily eight years later. I knew that eventually Jackie and Myrna would have to tell them the truth about how Auntie Miriam died. Now, of course, all five know. The Lau family lives in Hawaii; the Spurriers are back on the East Coast. They all take many plane trips routinely to visit us and other faraway places. When the children were small, how did Jackie and Myrna reassure them that airplane travel was safe? They explained that security had improved and the subject did not seem to come up any more.

Alena and Leah often asked to see pictures of Auntie Miriam as a child. They leafed through the albums. Miriam in her Red Riding Hood Halloween costume. Cuddling her cat and dog. Her fourth birthday party.

"Is Miriam in heaven?" Leah asked. Her mother assured her she is.

"Did you and Miriam ever have arguments?" Alena wanted to know.

"We sure did—lots of them." Those days Alena was flexing her nine-year-old's independence muscles, so she liked to hear that.

I can deal with all of this rationally now—most of the time. But in the beginning, well, that was a different story. For weeks after Miriam's death, my car became my private place of grief. Many mornings I'd pull into my office parking lot and sit in the car for ten minutes until I stopped crying and pulled myself together. My office was half a mile from BWI airport—so close that I'd see the planes coming and going every day. I couldn't get away from them. Their cold winking lights mocked me, reminding me that Miriam's plane didn't make it home. How I hated those winter nights, driving home in the sunset—the brilliant pinks and golds, the clouds haloed with reflected light. Miriam and I loved sunsets. We'd sit on a bench at our community dock, delighting in the flight of mallards and great blue herons as the sun settled over Cattail Creek.

Today I rarely cry in public. But those first two years I cried everywhere, especially in the supermarket, where I found myself bombarded with Mother's Day cards and birthday cards to daughters. At the mall, I walked into a shop where I'd bought Miriam a pumpkin-orange dress that she loved. I intended to browse, but suddenly started sobbing. Two young clerks watched me with alarmed looks. I backed out of the store without a word.

Time heals and it doesn't. The pain doesn't fizz and disappear like an Alka-Seltzer plopped into a glass of water. And I don't expect it to. I remember my Grandma Elizabeth coming to the hospital to visit my terminally ill mother. Elegant in her hat and gloves, ankles demurely crossed, Grandma sat next to Mother's bed day after day. After Mother died, Grandma's rosy cheeks turned pasty, her blue eyes dulled. She lived another decade, but she never recovered from her daughter's death.

Sigmund Freud lost his beloved twenty-six-year-old daughter to a sudden illness. Ten years later he wrote a friend: "Although we know that . . .the acute stage of mourning will subside, we also know that we shall remain inconsolable and will never find a substitute."

Miriam's death so shattered my father that he went to see the rabbi of the temple where our family had been members for forty-seven years. He sought answers as a bereaved grandfather, not as a psychoanalyst. It was only after Father died that I found out he'd visited the rabbi. The news shocked me because, although he was deeply Jewish and the son of Orthodox Jews, he hated organized religion, and after my mother died, he set foot in temple only for weddings and funerals. He consulted the rabbi, but couldn't tell me about it. I think he worried I would see it as a weakness. He wanted to be strong for me and to set an example of strength. Which he did. He practiced psychiatry until nineteen days before he died at eighty-six. If he'd been able to beat the cancer, he would have taken a computer course, "because I don't want to be left out of the mainstream," he told Larry and me.

I shouldn't have been surprised that he too was looking for answers, to make some sense out of the loss of his granddaughter. Miriam and Grandpa Saul were so dear to each other. She gave him strength, too. He learned from her—her eagerness to grow, to stretch her mind and explore. I once asked him:

"What keeps you going? What keeps you so optimistic?"

"Long ago," he said, "I decided I was going to live every day instead of die every day."

In some ways, I still can't accept the reality of Miriam's death. Sometimes I still wake up thinking this is preposterous, this couldn't have happened. I fantasize that she's still here. I construct a scenario that I had changed her to a different flight and brought her home safely. The most painful one, the absolute worst, is my wedding fantasy. I still can't pass a bridal shop without envisioning Miriam as a bride. I imagine the two of us flipping through bridal magazines. Or I hear a phone ring and it's my married Miriam calling to tell me she's pregnant. When she baby-sat for Rabbi and Fran Klensin's newborn son, I ambled across the street that Saturday night to see how things were going. Miriam answered the door with six-week-old Jacob slung on her hip, comfortably, as if he were her own second or third child. She would have made such a good mother. But I don't chastise myself for my fantasies. They float into my consciousness without invitation, unwelcome guests crashing my illusion of normalcy.

After Pan Am 103, the *Baltimore Jewish Times* raised astute questions: Why did the terrorists choose to plant a bomb on that particular flight? Because a large number of students were booked on it? Because the flight was scheduled so close to Christmas that the plane was expected to be full? Because a large number of Kosher meals had been ordered? Or was it because the chief Nazi hunter for the U.S. State Department was on board? To this day we have no answers. No official ones, at any rate.

So I began to search for answers of another kind—mystical answers. Now please know that I am a thoroughly pragmatic, unmystical person. Yet here I was, after Miriam died, stepping through the door of an uncharted dimension in my life.

We were hitting tennis balls in the hot Sunday sun, the four of us—Larry and I, Myrna and Tim. It felt so good to be hitting well. And a few minutes of rare freedom for the kids with their new baby boy, our second grandchild. Suddenly a soft chuckle came from outside the court, where Harriet, Tim's mother, was gently rocking Craig's stroller.

"Quick," she whispered, "you've got to see this." We all hurried over. Five-month-old Craig slept peacefully, his bare right foot resting on the stroller tray. On his chubby big toe sat a huge, exquisite monarch butterfly. We stood in silent awe as the butterfly lingered and lingered. A moment later, it gracefully darted off.

"It's Miriam," I said. "She's come to visit."

But my reaction embarrassed me. Was I behaving like a loony at a séance? Searching, searching, I dutifully flipped through my ever-growing stack of books on handling grief, yet gleaned no comfort. But one, written by a distinguished psychiatrist, caught my attention and I dove into it eagerly. It described cases of people who, under hypnosis, have recalled their former lives. The premise was that we live more than one life and this I can accept. Larry and I are so compatible that I'm convinced we knew each other in a previous life; on our first date I felt we'd been friends forever.

So I was getting hooked on this book. It documented cases of small children who were able to speak a foreign language fluently without ever having been taught it or even exposed to someone who spoke that language. The conclusion was that they learned it in a former life. Okay, that sounded plausible. But then it described the case of a woman who had come back to earth about eight times—and with a lousy life each time! I laughed out loud. Apparently she just wasn't cutting it either on earth or in the Hereafter, so the Great CEO in the Sky—or, more likely, the assistant manager on cloud 72—handed her her walking papers. Laid off from the Great Beyond. I suppose she was told: "You'll just have to keep going back until you get it right."

So that book didn't help. But I also discovered *A World Beyond* by psychic Ruth Montgomery. Our loved ones, she says, aren't dead and gone forever, they're merely on "the Other Side"; they make choices of their own and can come back in spirit to be with us at different times or to live an entirely fresh life. Somehow there's logic to this. It makes my reaction to the monarch butterfly seem less insane—even though Ms. Montgomery insists that humans don't change form in the afterlife. You can't come back as the family golden retriever. The butterfly is widely thought of as a symbol of a loved one's spirit.

But this concept of our loved ones being on the Other Side is both enlightening and scary. If Miriam is on the Other Side, does she eavesdrop on Larry and me at will? Is she smiling at us? Is she passing judgment on me? Probably. Or has my daughter already returned to earth to live another life of her own?

Guilt—I seem to have been born with a second skin of it. We had to find a new owner for Miriam's dog; the fleas had taken over our house. But nobody would take her. I had to return her to the SPCA, and they were furious with me. Months later, as I sat at my desk, a shrill bark assaulted my ears. New neighbors had moved in and their dog sounded just like Midnight. I brooded. God was punishing me for getting rid of her by reincarnating her in the dog next door.

I have been able to express my pain and find comfort in my friendship with Peggy and Ann. Nobody can truly understand except those who have lost daughters on that fateful flight. We meet for lunch when we can. And we talk about our feelings and how the little things hurt so much. It is with Ann and Peggy that I can rage at the seemingly invulnerable terrorists. Most important, we remember the special times we had with our daughters. We laugh a lot, too.

Six months after Miriam died a neighbor called to tell me her teenage son had broken his toe. She talked about it for ten minutes. I listened in silence, but when I hung up, I launched into a bitter argument with Larry.

"Miriam is dead and she's telling me about her son's toe? It isn't fair, why do I have to listen? My friends should stop telling me all this stuff."

Larry tried to explain. "They love you and loved Miriam, but they can't censor their every word. You need their friendship and they have their lives, too. Their children are what's important to them."

Anger bubbled up inside me like a malevolent hot spring. I ran upstairs to my desk and slammed myself into my chair. Burying my face in my arms, I burrowed into the basement of my mind. Was this to be my fate for the rest of my life—to listen stoically and grieve privately? Larry was right, of course, but back then I wasn't ready to accept it.

A year later, my neighbor and I talked about that particular phone conversation. Ironically, while she was telling me about the broken toe, she herself was wondering whether she should have said anything at all. Today my friends can tell me about their kids—now grown with wonderful children of their own. And now I tell them about Jackie and Myrna and our five grandchildren. I talk so exuberantly and for so long that I've even cautioned polite listeners: "You'd better unwind me or I'll go on for a week."

But I can be caught off guard—by a Facebook picture of one of Miriam's high school pals with her husband. And I'm overwhelmed by acute sadness all over again.

That's when I fall back down "the mountain," as my friend Ann calls it—the mountain of optimism and normalcy. Each day after Miriam died I clawed my way up, groping for footholds that would regain a measure of my life back, grasping at every twig and branch of goodness in my life to help me cope better. Miriam is not coming back. But I can't survive dwelling on that thought. I survive on the knowledge that God gave her to me for twenty years.

On her birthday we visit her grave and lay our pebbles down among the many already there. How I would love to plant heather, her favorite flower, beside her headstone. But it's an Orthodox Jewish cemetery and only green shrubs are allowed. I understand why flowers are prohibited. In Judaism we don't beautify death. Still, I've sometimes had a secret, almost overwhelming, urge to plant the heather anyway. I can visualize arriving one day to find the entire cemetery covered with a glorious purple blanket. And on her birthday we always do something special. Sometimes we go out to dinner with friends, and when we come home, I look up at the starry sky and ask God to keep Miriam safe for me.

Searching for meaning in my life, I've plunged into new diversions. Masterpiece Theatre's superb *Middlemarch* led me to the novel. Where had this book been all my life?

Watching the birds at our feeder, more than twenty species, just outside our kitchen window—now there's a lifetime of entertainment for you. Black-capped chickadees, Carolina wrens,

Northern cardinals, a tufted titmouse. The exquisitely colored blue jays, Nature's works of art. A flock of cedar waxwings stopped by, alighting on Miriam's apple tree. Every February in Honolulu, Larry and I take part in Audubon's Great Backyard Bird Count. At Magic Island we see as many as eight different species in half an hour.

We're members of Hawaii Opera Theatre and attend with friends and our daughter Jackie. Each season shines more brilliantly than the last. We've also discovered the thrilling Metropolitan Opera's live Saturday simulcasts at the Dole movie theater.

After a whole career mostly editing other authors, I began writing for myself, personal essays, many of them humorous.

Our grandson Craig, when he was five, asked me: "Rosemary, why do you laugh so much?"

"Because it makes me feel better," I said.

My biggest adventure by far: Larry and I embarked on a new career: writing fiction together. We published short stories and the Paco and Molly Mystery Series: *Boston Scream Pie*, *Hot Grudge Sunday* and *Locks and Cream Cheese*. Our newest novel is *Cry Ohana*, Adventure and Suspense in Hawaii ("ohana" is family in Hawaiian). We learn something new every day, and the harder we work the more fun we have. Keeping our characters in trouble keeps us out of trouble.

I've made another healing discovery: Our friends' children are now adults and have become our friends, too. One sent us postcards from her travels to China and Europe; these cards made my day, her thinking of us from distant continents. After I held a bridal shower for another young friend, she wrote me a letter in which she said, "I cherish your friendship." That was such a loving sentiment. We receive holiday photos of their children. There's a new and healthy dimension to all this. They are more special people in this world for me and Larry to care about.

It also dawned on me that, as an editor and writer, I should be using my own resources for Miriam's benefit. I began to publish her writings. Short stories, poems, essays, articles—in the *Washing-*

ton Post; Dramatics Magazine; New York Daily News; Art Times: A Cultural and Creative Journal; Kids' Byline; Soap Opera Stars; and Cricket, the magazine for children. For her short story "Outstanding in the Field," the *Cricket* editors added full-color illustrations by the noted artist Cat Bowman Smith.

Each time I published another of Miriam's pieces, I felt a tingle of triumph. Each time I saw her work in print, I felt I had immortalized her anew.

My days are buoyed up by her friends, who have showered us with poems written about her, a song composed for her, and a friend who named his new cat Luby.

Myrna and Jackie have been a great source of comfort to me. They call me their "stepmom" and at first I was careful to call them my stepdaughters. But it wasn't long before I yearned to call them "daughter." Would they be offended, I wondered. But they're not in the least, probably because I'm their friend and have never tried to take their mother's place. (Ironically, one of the many things we have in common is the fact that both of our mothers died of cancer at age forty-eight.)

I hate to admit it, but I'm a compulsive advice-giver—whether it's asked for or not. Maybe it grates on the girls at times, but they're both too diplomatic to say so. I did have one problem, though. At first I also wondered whether calling them "daughter" was in some way a betrayal of Miriam. I decided it wasn't. It's merely another symbol of how much I miss her.

Larry and I call the girls every week. Just talking to them cheers me up and makes me feel renewed, less deprived, less bereft. And talking to our grandchildren infuses me with happiness. Being able to talk about "our kids," "our girls" has given me a new lease on life. And Larry's willingness to share them with me is limitless, because that's the kind of person he is. Giving is a way of life for him.

Larry, with his humor and positive outlook, is my best friend, my mainstay. He's what we call a *mensch* in Yiddish, a loving, giving man. He appreciates my talking about Miriam and lets me cry as much as I need to. It's hard for him to see me suffering, but he never makes me feel that I should keep my anguish to myself because it makes him uncomfortable.

In the spring of 1993, Myrna and Tim called to tell us that they were moving from Maryland to Molokai, an outer island of Hawaii. They were both teachers and already had jobs. Tim, an athlete, wanted to be in a warm climate. Myrna wanted to be near her sister. But before the news was even out of Myrna's mouth, I began sobbing. *Here comes another loss*, I thought. The move was what the kids wanted and needed to do. But for three days I cried as if I'd lost another daughter.

Their move propelled Larry and me to take early retirement near the end of that year to spend the winters in Hawaii. We could manage it, we had our health, we'd be closer to our kids and our grandchildren would get to know us.

What I didn't count on was the shock of leaving my job. I had worked for thirty-four years, but only six at Westinghouse and I wasn't really geared to quit. A subtle new form of grieving settled over me as I thought about my friends and colleagues at work, my managers, whom I really liked, and the undeniable excitement and stimulation of the corporate climate. My identity had been wrenched from me; I was no longer a professional editor and writer. And catapulted into the quiet of our house, I now had too much time to brood about Miriam. She was dead almost five years, but that made no difference. It seemed like yesterday.

We arrived in balmy Hawaii with its caressing trade winds on December 1. Jackie and her family greeted us at the airport with fragrant plumeria leis and hugs and kisses. But as we neared December 21, the fifth anniversary of Pan Am 103, an additional sense of isolation overtook me.

I have always been deeply affected by the passage of seasons. Every December for as long as I can remember, I would weave my way through rush hour traffic in darkness, gratefully aware on the twenty-first of the month that the days would now start growing longer. But now December 21 is a sinister day. The weeks leading up to it loom heavy as I helplessly rehash the night Miriam died. I want to forget, but the horror wraps around me like a python and smothers me with its reality. The shortest day of the year, the longest night, the onset of winter. On December 21, 1988, winter settled into my soul.

December of 1993 was particularly painful. The families of Pan Am 103 were meeting with President Clinton at Arlington National Cemetery in Virginia to lay the cornerstone for a memorial. The bombing was considered an act of terrorism against the government of the United States. The memorial would be a Scottish "cairn," a fifteen-foot-high monument of 270 red brick-shaped stones, one for each victim, donated by the Scottish government and mined from a quarry near Lockerbie. Never had I felt so alone. I wanted to be with Ann and Peggy and the other families to mourn our children. So what did I do to console myself?

I walked around the corner from our apartment to a Korean beauty parlor to get my hair done. On December 21 at 10 a.m. I engaged in a comically unsolemn conversation with the lady proprietor.

"My hair won't stay set in this tropical climate," I complained.

"Of course," she lectured me. "Wrong hairdo for Hawaii. I cut it short, much better, no more set."

"Really?" I asked uneasily. But she had already started snipping. Moments later, I looked like a fifty-eight-year-old pixie.

That night I confided in Jackie: "My first new hairdo in fourteen years. Miriam encouraged me." Then I blushed for saying something so weird.

But she laughed. "Like Miriam was telling you, 'Mom, go for it!'"

Jackie's reaction amazed me. She didn't think I was crazy. Her complete understanding washed over me like a gentle wave. It was okay for me to be in Hawaii instead of at Arlington. On December 21, as much as we could manage it, Miriam and I were together after all.

I spend a good and satisfying share of my life with my nose in dictionaries and my thesaurus. In writing this book, I've made a discovery. There aren't many synonyms in the English language for "cry." One can say "weep" or "sob" or "shed tears," or "mourn," but then you start running out of words. Maybe there's a message in this, a basic truth that emerges through thousands of years of our language's evolution. Maybe after we allow ourselves all the crying we need to—or perhaps despite the crying that helps us—we need to turn our attention, no matter how much we hurt, to living the best way we can.

In *A Grief Observed*, C.S. Lewis writes about the death of his young wife:

> Passionate grief does not link us with the dead but cuts us off from them. . . .It is just at those moments when I feel least sorrow—getting into my morning bath is one of them—that H. rushes upon my mind in her full reality... Not, as in my worst moments, all foreshortened and patheticized and solemnized by miseries, but as she is in her own right. That is good and tonic.

The oddest thing about that quote is that Miriam recorded it in one of her London diaries. Why, in a time of such happiness, was she drawn to this sentiment? I get chills when I read it, because it speaks directly to me. And it confirms my feeling that she had a mystical side to her.

CHAPTER 13

"This Day Is Mine"

IN OCTOBER 1993, I reached a milestone. I published an article in *McCall's* entitled "Please Remember My Daughter." The day of publication gave me a sense of achievement like no other since she died. Now millions of readers throughout the world knew about my child. The article ended with Miriam's own words, her personal guidelines for her life.

The force of her personality came through with such power that the response to the article surprised even me. A high school senior in Maryland concluded her graduation valedictory address with Miriam's words. A woman in Israel invited Larry and me to visit. A teacher in Ohio called to say Miriam's story had given her courage and strength—strength that she sorely needed, because this single Caucasian woman had adopted an African-American baby and much of her family had disowned her afterward. The editor-in-chief of *McCall's*, Kate White (now editor-in-chief of *Cosmopolitan*), wrote to me on September 19, 1993:

"Reading about Miriam has had a very big effect on my life—I really carry her wisdom with me every day now. I had gotten away from seeing the joy of each day and she has restored my spirit. What a fabulous legacy."

What were Miriam's words that stoked the fires of so many people? They were her own prescription for living, her personal philosophy, which I myself only discovered in one of her London notebooks. It is such profound advice that it speaks to all of us. But it speaks especially to me. With these words, my daughter has taken me by the hand and led me into a healing place:

There are times when the 'poor me' mood is upon us; we're overwhelmed by all the troubles we have to face. This is especially likely to happen when we have begun to try to change our thinking about ourselves and our relation to others. We may, at first, become too analytical and try to solve too much at once. For this frame of mind there is an almost infallible prescription: to empty our minds of all thoughts but one—today and how to use it. This day is mine. It is unique. Nobody in the world has one exactly like it. It holds the sum of all my past experience and all my future potential.

A Photo Album

**All the following photos can be found in color
on Rosemary and Larry's web site:
www.magicile.com/books/miriamsworldphotos**

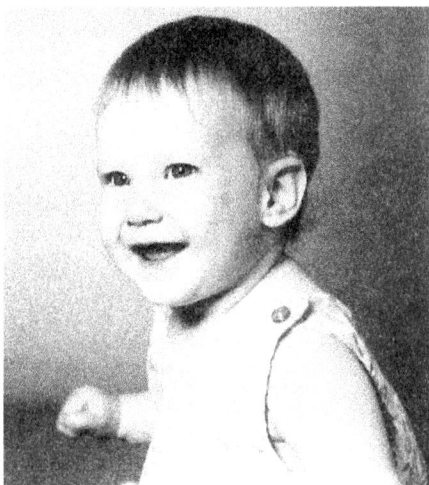

Miriam at ages four months and three years.

At age four, the two of us at Hershey Park Zoo, Lancaster, PA

Kindergarten: wearing Greek jumper that Grandpa Saul Pollack brought back from an international psychoanalytic convention.

At age eight, hamming it up with her cousin Marlene Pollack (right), Grandpa Saul and his golden retriever, Jerome. The girls are wearing tams that Grandpa brought back from Scotland.

Her first puppy. She named him Shane Henry.

With Cuddles.

With Hoppy.

Miriam with Midnight, who was so pitch black
we constantly stumbled over her.

At thirteen she played basketball and clarinet and ran the mile.

Standing by her ceramic mask in a community art show. She's saying, "Mom, let's get this over with before any of my friends see me."

Visiting MGM in Los Angeles—on the set of "CHiPS" with actor Robert Pine and Miriam's friend Wendy Moser.

131

The Red Delicious apple tree she planted at age five.

At thirteen, she stuck this board in our maple tree and called it
The Office. "I'm going to the office, Mom!"

On vacation with her stepbrother, Chris Spencer.

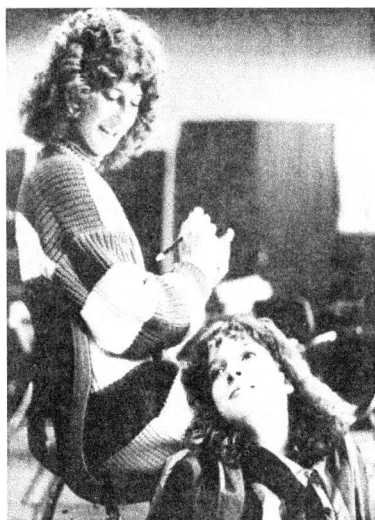

Photo by *The Capital*

Severna Park High School Senior Class Play,
rehearsing with friend Bonnie.

133

The Capital

Youth

MONDAY
March 10, 1986 — Page 8

GREASY KIDSTUFF

Students say play ban is censorship

By JENNIFER TAWES
and MIRIAM WOLFE
Severna Park Senior High

"Grease," the second longest running Broadway musical and blockbuster movie, will not be presented at Severna Park High School this year despite a unanimous vote of the drama club.

The principal of Severna Park High, Oliver Wittig, felt that the play was inappropriate for use in a public school because it advocated "sex, booze and rock 'n' roll."

These writers are filing a grievance over the play, contending students and parents were inadequately represented on the board that made the decision.

Severna Park High School's Drama Club submitted the musical "Grease" to

should be permitted to produce "One Flew Over The Cuckoo's Nest."

The state board's decision was made with the hope that "the immediate issues presented in this appeal will hopefully not recur."

Wittig's decision to reject "Grease" is in opposition to the state Board of Education's call for consistency. This lack of consistency within the county is easily remedied.

One former Severna Park MOI committee member offered the solution that "the county should be consistent in its bylaws, while still maintaining MOI committees in each school." The school's MOI function would then be to alter, if necessary, the objectionable scenes to suit the community's standards.

Moreover, the MOI committee should operate by holding meetings at which oral arguments are presented, rather than simply submitting individual opinions without any discussion. The MOI

GUEST WRITERS

MIRIAM WOLFE
Drama Club President

JENNIFER TAWES
Drama Club member

Photos by J. Henson

An activist at seventeen—taking a stand against high school play censorship.

134

A Syracuse friend took this endearing photo
during their sophomore year.

My three girls, May 1987. With me, from left: Jackie Mild Lau, Myrna Mild Spurrier (receiving her master's in art education) and Miriam.

Syracuse University, sophomore year—the two of us in her dorm room.

Makeup magic.

Performing at Darien Lake, NY.

As the shrill, fluttery Mrs Spenser in *Anne of Green Gables,*
sophomore year at Syracuse U.

137

At a London cafe, Miriam with three friends—(clockwise from lower left) her flatmate Jessica Genick and friends Christine Venier and Anne Husak.

In Amsterdam, the Netherlands.

On a three-day trip to Wales.

Miriam's grave in Annapolis, Maryland.

The memorial wall at Syracuse University.

The Garden of Remembrance in Lockerbie, Scotland.

Our plaque for Miriam in the Garden of Remembrance,
Lockerbie, Scotland.

At Arlington National Cemetery the memorial is a Scottish cairn
—270 stones, one for each victim, mined from a quarry near Lockerbie
and donated by the Scottish people.

141

Syracuse University
REMEMBRANCE QUILT

HONORING THE VICTIMS OF PAN AM 103

10th Anniversary • December 21,1998

Miriam's block on the Remembrance Quilt.

Miriam, Continued:
Love, Lessons and Politics

(The Year 2000 and Beyond)

A Brief Timeline

April 5, 1986. Libya bombs La Belle discotheque in West Berlin, Germany, popular with American service personnel. Two American soldiers are killed, more than 90 others injured.

April 15, 1986. President Reagan orders the bombing of Tripoli, Libya's capital city, in retaliation for La Belle.

July 3, 1988. The USS *Vincennes* mistakenly shoots down Iran Air Flight 655, misidentifying the airbus as an Iranian Air Force F-14.

December 21, 1988. A terrorist bomb destroys Pan Am Flight 103 over Lockerbie, Scotland, killing all 259 on board and 11 on the ground—among them, my daughter, Miriam Luby Wolfe, and 34 other Syracuse University students.

November 6, 1990. Spearheaded by the Pan Am 103 families, the Federal Aviation Security Improvement Act becomes law.

Early 1990s. Scholarships and awards are established in Miriam's memory in Maryland.

1991. The U.S. indicts two Libyan intelligence agents for the bombing of Pan Am 103.

February 26, 1993. In New York City, a bomb explodes in the World Trade Center parking garage, killing 6 and injuring more than 1,000.

1996. President Clinton signs the Terrorist Prevention Act into law. It amends the Foreign Sovereign Immunities Act to allow U.S. citizens to sue governments that sponsor terrorism.

1998. The U.S. and Britain agree to conduct the trial of the two bombers under Scottish law with Scottish judges. Libya accepts in theory but refuses to turn over the suspects.

1998. Syracuse University establishes its Remembrance Scholars Program. The Remembrance Quilt makes its debut.

May 2000. The trial begins in the Netherlands at Kamp Zeist, a former American Air Force base.

January 31, 2001. The Scottish Court pronounces Megrahi "guilty," Fhimah "not guilty."

September 11, 2001. Hijackers commandeer four airplanes: two destroy the World Trade Center in New York City; a third attacks the Pentagon; the fourth, meant for either the White House or the U.S. Capitol, crashes in a field near Shanksville, Pennsylvania.

March 14, 2002. Megrahi's appeal of his sentence is denied.

2003. Under pressure from the United States, Great Britain and the United Nations, Moammar Gadhafi renounces terrorism and agrees to dismantle his nuclear weapons program.

2005. Libya accepts responsibility for the bombing of Pan Am Flight 103.

2006. The U.S. government removes Libya from its list of states that sponsor terrorism.

2007. Libya and Vietnam are elected to serve two-year terms on the United Nations Security Council.

August 20, 2009. The Scottish Minister of Justice frees mass murderer Megrahi "on compassionate grounds"—not to a Libyan prison, but to his family.

CHAPTER 14

Tulips on Trial

WHEN YOU PLANT TULIP BULBS IN OCTOBER, you take a lot on faith. Will they reward you with gorgeous blooms in the spring? Or will the squirrels get there first, burrowing in, digging up the bulbs and feasting on them?

For Larry and me, this endeavor was akin to buying a lottery ticket. We're not clever gardeners. Nevertheless, my fragile hopes ran high in October 2000, when we diligently planted fifty bulbs in the modest flower bed fronting our house.

We bought our pack of bulbs in Alsmeer, the Netherlands, home of the largest flower auction in the world. But these were not your ordinary bulbs. Our precious tulips came fraught with symbolism and represented a grievous journey. We bought them a week before traveling to Kamp Zeist, southeast of Amsterdam. We were headed there to attend the trial of the two Libyan terrorists: Abdel Basset al-Megrahi and Lamen Khalifa Fhimah. They were indicted by the United States and Great Britain in 1991 for planting the bomb on Pan Am Flight 103.

In the Alsmeer gift shop, as I waited to pay for our bulbs, my thoughts drove me down two avenues: the romance of buying tulips in Holland and their emotional context on the eve of the trial. These captivating flowers would be more than a souvenir. They would stand, year after year, as a memorial to Miriam.

So stubbornly had I fixed on these profound implications

that I neglected to ask the gift shop ladies just where it is that you plant tulip bulbs. In the shade? In full sun?

Larry and I learned the answer by default. Across the street from our house, the sunny side, our neighbors' tulips bloom weeks before ours. Oh, dear. Tulips belong in full sun. We, on the north side, get only half-sun. Sometimes only quarter-sun. In the winter, snow sits on our front lawn longer than on anyone else's in the neighborhood.

In mid-April 2001, the first bud popped open. I leaned over it and stared in dismay. So skinny. Would they all be like that? Do tulip blossoms get larger, more robust each day? Or, if they're born underdeveloped, do they stay pathetic, unable to catch up? Amazingly enough, each day new blooms greeted me. And with each one, I rushed back into the house and announced their status to Larry. "We have seven, dear. Come look!" I shouted. "We're up to twelve!" I cheered. I counted the blooms obsessively at least once a day.

Our fifty brave bulbs gave birth to sixty-four blooms. And they all progressed to a hearty cup shape. Not earth-shattering, not prize-winning, but respectable. I took pictures to capture their beauty: a blaze of yellow bursting inside a scarlet cup; a white star nestling in velvety purple. Each day as I bounded out of the house for the morning paper, I greeted our tulips as if they'd be with me forever.

THE TRIAL of the two Libyans took place in the Netherlands before a Scottish court at Kamp Zeist, a former American Air Force base. The United Nations had negotiated this unusual arrangement with Libyan leader Moammar Gadhafi, who demanded that the trial be held in a neutral country. A concrete building at Kamp Zeist was transformed into a modern courthouse with a special secluded lounge for the victims' families. We attended the trial—already in its sixth month—for a week in October 2000, along with twelve other Pan Am family members. Before leaving for Europe, I cried for days, filled with anxiety over the prospect of facing the murderers of my daughter. Nevertheless, Larry and I realized there would be a cathartic benefit to seeing them in the flesh and showing our support for their prosecution.

Our first morning, as our minibus approached the courthouse, we saw formidable but reassuring security. High chain-link fences with barbed wire. Scottish guards in blue, white and black uniforms with Kevlar vests and automatic weapons. Entering the courtroom for the first time sent a chill down my spine. A massive, floor-to-ceiling bulletproof glass wall separated the spectators from the court itself. Just beyond the glass, on the left, the defendants sat in an elevated box flanked by two guards. Directly below them, the defense team occupied two rows of tables and chairs. Facing them along the right wall was the Crown's prosecution team, including several U.S. State Department advisers. The three presiding judges, plus one alternate, occupied the "bench," a massive raised dais under the Scottish court crest.

I stared at the two men accused of mass murder, the men who had destroyed the life of my beautiful Miriam. A wave of fear shot through me. Not because they looked like monsters, not because I felt physically threatened. But because they looked so ordinary. Author Hannah Arendt, writing about Nazi war criminal Adolph Eichmann, described "the banality of evil." I had not understood the concept before. Now I did.

The spectator side of the glass wall held upholstered theater-style chairs and headphones for translations. We family members were seated in the large center section near the front. The physical closeness of these twelve warm, loving people—strangers to Larry and me before the trial—gave me strength. We shared so much, belonging to an involuntary club as victims of terrorism. We shared memories of our loved ones; the pain of our altered lives; our feelings toward the accused; the splintered and sometimes biased media; and the sway of the trial itself.

At the back of the courtroom sat a group of observers of varying ethnic origins, representing the United Nations War Crimes Commission. The defendants' families and supporters, numbering only a few, occupied the smaller section on the left. My eyes unwillingly met the angry gaze of a large swarthy woman wearing the traditional black head scarf: Megrahi's wife. Her outfit, a long print skirt and jacket, could have come from Sears or J.C. Penney. She sat with their two children, perhaps pre-teens, who fidgeted in their chairs. A stream of heavy emotions tugged at me. The defendants have families? Loved ones? How could men so zealously evil, deliberately killing innocents, even babies, have genuine feelings? Doesn't ice water run in their veins?

We were warned to use only the restrooms in our family lounge, not the general one for trial visitors out in the corridor, because we might find ourselves in a confrontation.

It is widely believed that Scotland is one of the most pro-defendant countries in the world. The *Washington Post* reported that a special chef would prepare meals for the two defendants. The court also granted them a prayer room and exercise room. Did Oklahoma City bombers Timothy McVeigh and Terry McNichols—or any other mass murderer in an American prison—ever receive such amenities?

ON JANUARY 31, 2001, the three Scottish judges pronounced Megrahi "Guilty!" and sentenced him to twenty years before he would be eligible for parole—the longest sentence allowed under Scottish law. We family members were outraged and frustrated. It was quickly pointed out that a sentence of twenty years meant Megrahi would serve less than one month for each of the 270 victims. Adding to our dismay, Fhimah was declared "Not guilty." The prosecution could not directly link him to the purchase of the timer circuit board that triggered the bomb. We felt sick to read that he flew home to a hero's welcome.

Nevertheless, a small measure of gratitude swept over Larry and me. At least we got one conviction. Evil had not won out entirely. Most of the families felt as we did. Nothing would bring our children back, but after twelve years, the verdict gave us a particle of justice.

Our sense of gratitude did not last long. As for peace of mind? Forget it.

SEPTEMBER 11, 2001: Xian, China, on our Grand Circle tour. Larry and I awoke early, still tasting the exhilaration of our previous day's visit to the terra cotta warriors. The phone rang. It was Marty, our friend and fellow traveler in the hotel room next door. "Turn on CNN!" he shouted.

The terrorist attacks on American soil had changed our world for the worst—again. Shock waves and fear reverberated through our tour group. Frantic phone calls to a wife working in the Pentagon. A son on Wall Street. Grandchildren in western Pennsylvania. Our fellow travelers knew how my daughter died and whispered among themselves: "How's Rosemary? Is she okay?"

Outwardly, yes, I was calm. Too calm. In fact, at first I felt almost nothing. My brain shifted into reverse, disconnecting me from reality. To make things worse, the Chinese government took CNN off the air. The full impact of 9/11 stubbornly escaped me. We were halfway around the world, not in our kitchen in Severna Park, inches from the phone and the cold Pan Am voice that told me, at 12:30 a.m. on December 22, 1988, "M. Wolfe is on the manifest."

During the following days, the enormity of the 9/11 attacks seeped in. Our tour ended in Hong Kong. Inside the airport, tall Chinese soldiers patrolled with automatic weapons poised, ready to fire. A spasm cramped my belly—not from the vicious abdominal cramps that my Crohn's Disease inflicts, but from a sense of hopelessness and dread. Even today I feel haunted, thinking of the hundreds of brave firefighters and other heroic souls who perished trying to save lives during the destruction of the Twin Towers, the Pentagon and Flight 93.

The Pan Am 103 families had spearheaded a potent new law, the Aviation Security Improvement Act of 1990. Was it all for nothing? For centuries, philosophers have warned that those who ignore history are doomed to repeat it. How could the United

States Government have failed so miserably to anticipate 9/11?

Michael Chertoff became the first Secretary of the Department of Homeland Security, created in 2002 in response to 9/11. He has provided some cogent answers. Every December 21, a commemoration service is held at the Pan Am 103 memorial cairn in Arlington National Cemetery, in Arlington, Virginia. On December 21, 2007, then-Secretary Chertoff was the keynote speaker and said:

> . . .The sad truth is that what followed Lockerbie was not a period of sober remembrance and reappraisal. What followed Lockerbie was a time of tremendous amnesia and self-delusion. Less than a year after Lockerbie, the Berlin Wall came down and two years later, the Soviet Union fell and hundreds of millions of people were liberated from the tyranny of Communism. As the world rightly celebrated, Lockerbie was all but forgotten. There was even talk about the end of history, but columnist Charles Krauthammer got it right when he said that in the years that followed, we took a 'holiday from history.' The terrorists, however, took no such holiday, but worked overtime to launch future attacks.
>
> In 1993, they bombed the World Trade Center. By the mid-Nineties, they had almost succeeded in blowing up the Lincoln and Holland tunnels. In 1996, they attacked our forces in Khobar Towers [Saudi Arabia]. In 1998, ten years after Lockerbie, Osama Bin Laden openly declared war, commanding his followers 'to kill the Americans and their allies—civilian and military—in any country where it is possible to do it.' And then came the African Embassy bombings, the USS *Cole* attack and finally, September 11th.
>
> By choosing the primrose path of complacency borne out of euphoria, by forgetting the horror of Lockerbie, and by failing to respond fully to the evil done that

day, we arrived at the deadly destination of September 11, 2001. . . .

THE APPEAL: When you lose a child, there's no such thing as closure—not for me, anyway. But with the verdict of "Guilty!" at Kamp Zeist, I naively assumed we had arrived at legal closure. I should have known better. Megrahi launched his appeal immediately. But first came a hearing to decide whether the appeal should be allowed to go forward.

Back home in Severna Park, Larry and I followed the proceedings on the secure web site established for the Flight 103 families by the U.S. Department of Justice Office for Victims of Crime. Each day, as we printed out summaries of the hearing, I agonized over every shred of the defense's arguments.

On October 15, 2001, the five new Scottish judges announced their decision. I was horrified and ranted to Larry: "It's only a month after 9/11! How can they allow the appeal to go forward?" I paced the kitchen floor, my voice strident. "The trial lasted nine months and the Libyans had eleven years to prepare their case. Why is Megrahi being given such leeway? It's shameful!" My husband had no answer.

The appeal trial lasted thirteen months. As we read the summaries each day, Larry remained coolly confident that each new piece of "evidence" produced in such volume by the defense was flimsy. I agreed with him intellectually, but my stomach knotted up with doubt. What if the conviction were overturned? What if no one was made to pay for Miriam's death?

On March 14, 2002, at 5:30 a.m. Eastern Standard Time, the five Scottish judges announced their verdict: "We have concluded that none of the grounds of the appeal is well founded. The appeal will accordingly be refused. This brings proceedings to an end."

At the time, Larry and I were spending the winter in Hawaii. Holding our breath, our eyes transfixed on CNN, we heard the verdict. Appeal denied. We did not whoop and cheer. No. We fell into each other's arms and wept.

I could breathe again. But I still felt a lurking reserve—until much later that day, when I logged onto the *New York Times* on-line and read "Megrahi was flown to Scotland late tonight to begin his sentence there." That single line somehow liberated me, released me. It was the first tangible news, something I could grasp and clutch and cling to. Megrahi was now physically caged in a Victorian-era prison in Glasgow. According to Reuters news service, Barlinnie has borne the reputation (until recently) as Scotland's toughest jail, administered under "Dickensian conditions." Yes! The bomber was being punished for his unspeakable mass murder of 270 innocent victims.

Megrahi, the former security chief of Libyan Arab Airlines in Malta, is of course only one man. Although Fhimah was acquitted, the U.S. Government believes he, too, was guilty. And it is universally known that the two men did not act on their own, that the order to bomb Pan Am 103 came from Gadhafi himself. For many years, Libya was known to sponsor terrorism.

A civil suit filed by a group of Flight 103 families against Libya was now settled. The civil action included the cornerstone condition that Moammar Gadhafi take public responsibility for the bombing and renounce terrorism. In 2003, under pressure from the United States, Great Britain and the United Nations, he renounced his country's terrorism and agreed to dismantle his nuclear weapons program. In 2005, at last, Libya accepted responsibility for the bombing of Flight 103.

We returned home from Hawaii in time for our darling tulips to perform for their second season. As we wheeled our luggage up the walk, I cheered. "Larry, they're coming up!"

Well, sort of. A few scrawny leaves greeted us. In the next few weeks, I expected them to burst forth with buds and blooms even stronger and healthier than the first year's. I expected them to join Larry and me in celebrating and symbolizing our victory.

But April and May came and went. In our entire flower bed, only twelve clumps of leaves appeared. Twelve clumps. Not one tulip! There the leaves stood: lonely, straggly, disheartened. And surrounding them, I discovered dents in the soil. Dents and deep holes. Larry leaned down and studied them. "Hmm," he said. "Must be the squirrels." I nodded, too disappointed to agree aloud.

Several years ago, we planted gerbera daisies and the flowers popped out in blazing yellows, oranges and purples. By the next morning, each dazzling bloom had disappeared. Rabbits had devoured them for breakfast. After a week of this, I got so frustrated that I roared across the highway to our local garden center and bought a bunch of silk roses, complete with fake dew on their delicate petals. For two whole summers, our friends raved about our stunning roses. Until they tried to smell them.

So . . . after a day of pondering the dents in the garden, I could visualize what must have happened. Our resident squirrels undoubtedly followed the Libyans' trial and appeal. In my mind's eye, I could see them gathered in a huddle, their plumed tales quivering.

"Listen up," the head honcho squirrel said. "The trial's over. The appeal's over. Let's eat!"

My daughter had an unquenchable optimism and vision—far greater than my own—to explore her talents, to soak up experiences and to seek out new ones. In a paper she wrote for a dance class at Syracuse, she said, "To be a true artist, one must challenge and defy convention, remain open-minded and always continue to learn."

It's time to take my cue from Miriam. Instead of brooding about spring blooms and what will come up or not come up, I think of our precious Dutch bulbs and pack them away in a corner of my memory. I smile at the squirrels prancing along our maple branches. My decision is made. I jump in my car and head for the garden center. They have exquisite silk tulips.

CHAPTER 15

270 Betrayals

THE INSIDIOUS tremors began in 2008, foretelling a virtual earthquake. Bomber Abdel Basset Ali Megrahi was diagnosed with prostate cancer and petitioned the Scottish court to return him to Libya on compassionate grounds. Incarcerated at the time in Scotland's Greenock prison, he then also applied for bail.

The Crown rigorously opposed the bail application. Bail, or "interim liberation" in Scotland, is different from bail in the U.S.; it doesn't involve money. It is decided on the basis of the offense and whether the prisoner might re-offend.

The tremors grew to rumblings, reminding Larry and me that the Scottish justice system contains a dangerous, indigenous fault line: extreme leniency. Megrahi, from the time of his conviction, had a TV set in his cell and access to a kitchen. He received regular visits from his wife, who was living for awhile nearby in a residence paid for by the Libyan government.

Compounding our anxiety, Megrahi filed a second appeal to reverse his conviction. Another painful fissure that cracked my composure.

On the web site established for the Pan Am families to follow the proceedings, it was reported that ". . . .The Scottish Criminal Cases Review Commission has identified five reasons which led it to believe that a miscarriage of justice may have occurred. [We] . . . hold that the appellant is entitled to have his stated grounds of appeal decided by the court on their respective merits. . . ." A month later, the Scottish court denied bail, but would consider a second application at a later date if Megrahi's health deteriorated.

On November 17, 2008, the U.K. and Libya signed a Prisoner Transfer Agreement. It would give prisoners the opportunity to complete their sentences in their own countries. The Scottish Government had asked the U.K. to exclude Megrahi or anyone else convicted of the Pan Am 103 bombing. The exclusion was not granted. Ten months later, the world would discover that the U.K. and Libya negotiated this treaty specifically for the benefit of one prisoner: Megrahi.

Scottish Cabinet Secretary of Justice Kenny MacAskill alone would be making the final decision and had three options to consider: (1) grant Megrahi early release—meaning his freedom—on compassionate grounds; (2) approve the Prisoner Transfer Agreement, which would allow him to return to Libya to complete his sentence; (3) or keep him in the Scottish prison to serve out his sentence.

As 2009 unfolded, these developments set the stage for a firestorm of protest. Frank Duggan, president of the Flight 103 families' group, steadfastly led us with this declaration, adopted by the board on March 29:

> The 270 victims of the bombing of Pan Am Flight 103 never had the chance to die in their homes with their families at their sides. We, the families and friends of those 270 victims, did not have the opportunity to say goodbye to them, thus we do understand the personal pain of Megrahi and his family. Nevertheless, Mr. Megrahi has been convicted of murdering all 270 victims on Pan Am Flight 103. He will receive the same medical treatment whether or not he is in a Scottish prison. . . .Compassionate release for Mr. Megrahi should not be contemplated.

On May 6, *The Scottish Law Reporter* explained that Megrahi's second appeal against conviction would be dropped if his transfer to a Libyan jail took place.

On July 9, a group of Pan Am family members held a transatlantic video conference, allowing them to speak directly to the Scottish Justice Minister to voice their distress and opposition.

On July 14, a meticulous factual appeal came from the two leaders in the Pan Am investigation task force: Richard A. Marquise, FBI Special Agent in Charge (retired) and Stuart Henderson, Detective Chief Superintendent. They ended with this compelling statement:

> Mr. Megrahi has spent approximately fourteen days in jail for each victim of the Lockerbie attack. The eight judges . . . came to the same conclusion the rest of us did—Mr. Megrahi was guilty of murder. His current health situation does not change that . . .

A month later, on August 14, a U.S. Senate delegation met with Libyan leaders in Tripoli. Senators John McCain, Joseph Lieberman, Susan Collins and Lindsay Graham strongly opposed Megrahi's release. That same day, Megrahi asked the court to abandon his appeal against conviction because he could not be considered for transfer or release if he was still appealing.

This was a bad sign. Something was up. On August 16, *The Scotsman.com* articulated our fears in an article entitled "Megrahi Must Stay":

> Is Scottish justice negotiable? That is the disturbing question many people will ask as suspicions of a back-room deal to free convicted Lockerbie bomber Megrahi are fuelled by the murky rumours, leaks and political interventions complicating his case. It was the abandonment of Megrahi's second appeal on Friday that really set the alarm

bells ringing. . . .It sent a strong signal that a deal was being brokered. That signal was received loud and clear in Washington: within hours, U.S. Secretary of State Hillary Clinton was on the telephone to Scottish Justice Secretary Kenny MacAskill. "He was brought to trial. He had a fair trial. He was convicted. He's serving his time. And we think he should stay in jail."

This newspaper's stated view is that Megrahi should serve out his time in prison . . .

On August 17, MacAskill received an impassioned letter from seven U.S. senators, including Edward M. Kennedy and John F. Kerry. Senator Kennedy, suffering from terminal brain cancer, signed the letter just eight days before he died. The senators reminded MacAskill that, in 1998, the governments of both the United States and the U.K. had made a crucial agreement: that the bombers, if convicted, would serve their entire sentence in Scotland. Now that commitment was in danger of unraveling.

THE PREVIOUS week, several local reporters came to our house with their photographers, asking our thoughts on the forthcoming decision. These were hours of high anxiety for Larry and me. We had Miriam's photos and *Miriam's Gift* spread out on the dining room table. We had houseguests—our daughters, Jackie and Myrna, and four of our five grandchildren. Their timing couldn't have been more perfect; Larry and I desperately needed their moral support. Photographers took pictures of all of us together.

Shortly before midnight, on August 20, 2009, the dreaded e-mail flooded my screen—with MacAskill's decision attached. Like an earthquake measuring 8.5 on the Richter scale, it was the most destructive, the most cataclysmic. Larry was already asleep. I rushed to our room to wake him. The Scottish Minister of Justice had released the Pan Am Flight 103 bomber "on compassionate grounds" because of his supposedly terminal prostate cancer.

"Release" did not mean transfer to a Libyan prison. It meant his freedom! Larry wrapped me in his arms and I cried, my hot tears dampening his shoulder. But not for long.

Racing back to my desk, I scribbled notes, random thoughts full of rage and disbelief, on what I would tell the media. I had a foreboding about the next morning when reporters would be calling. Would I be able to keep my cool? Or would I totally lose it and rant and rave?

The news hit the world just after midnight on August 21. The phone started ringing before breakfast. As Miriam's mother, my name was now prominent. All of us Pan Am families had again become celebrities—and again for the most grotesque reason.

I wore black. At 11 a.m. reporters and their photographers began crowding into our living room, in order of their appointments: six Baltimore and Washington TV stations; the *Baltimore Sun*; Associated Press; *USA Today*; and the *Washington Post*. I did phone interviews with *The* (Annapolis) *Capital*; the Fox News Network; WBAL Radio; *The News of the World* (Scotland) and *The Daily Express* (U.K.). Kristen at the Canadian Broadcasting Company in Toronto called after she saw us on the *Washington Post* web site.

One reporter asked me, "How do you feel?" The question had to be posed, but still, it was almost a caricature. If the context hadn't been so disturbing and of such worldwide consequence, I would have laughed. That night I remembered Woody Allen's *Bananas*, where a reporter asks a guerrilla soldier who lies dying on the church steps, "Are you upset?"

Of course, my answer was "I feel awful." Thank heaven for the notes I wrote at midnight. I told reporter Susan Reimer of the *Baltimore Sun*: "I'm a writer, but there are not enough adjectives in the dictionary to express my horror and disgust. I'm experiencing a whole new kind of grief." The front-page article, in print and on the *Sun's* web site, was read even by our friends in Hawaii. Susan's colleague, photographer Barbara Haddock Taylor, took lots of pictures. One that I particularly love was a close-up of the antique locket-pin I was wearing containing Miriam's picture at age thirteen—with a mischievous braces-filled smile.

What a small world we live in. Susan had interviewed me and written a beautiful article on *Miriam's Gift* when the first edition came out.

We welcomed John Rydell, of Baltimore's Fox 45 TV. John and I are both members of the Society of Professional Journalists. He reminded us that our Baltimore chapter had held a holiday party and we had brought Miriam with us. He remembered her— and on this grim day, that made me happy.

AP reporter Brian Witte brought photographer Steve Ruark, Syracuse University class of 2000.

Roosevelt Leftwich, of Baltimore's Channel 2, asked if his photographer, Manny Locke, could take a picture of Miriam's apple tree. In our backyard, I confessed to Roosevelt that the tree looked pretty dilapidated. He cheered me up. It had aged remarkably well, he said, considering that such fruit trees don't usually last thirty-six years. And those knobby lumps on the trunk? Not unusual. Hah!

Later in the day, I received a call from Neil Mitchell, host of the radio program *The Morning Show* in Melbourne, Australia. He asked me to speak for his live audience. I quoted from MacAskill's bizarre rationalization: "Al-Megrahi did not show his victims any comfort or compassion. They were not allowed to return to the bosom of their families to see out their lives, let alone their dying days. But that alone is not a reason for us to deny compassion to him and his family in his final days."

I swallowed hard to keep my voice from cracking as I spoke to those listeners halfway around the world: "How could it not be enough of a reason? MacAskill is saying that the life and comfort of one state-sponsored terrorist is worth more than the lives of all 270 of our innocent loved ones!"

I GET a lump in my throat the size of a hard-boiled egg when I recall how kind and sensitive all the media were to us. And I'm touched beyond words at how much space they devoted to Miriam's pictures and my book cover. It took me three weeks, but I managed to send thank-you e-mails. Larry and I received this gratifying response from Brian Witte: "Thank you both for speaking with us under such difficult circumstances. Your poise and dignity enormously enhanced the ramifications of the decision."

WHEN Larry and I published *Boston Scream Pie*, our third Paco and Molly Mystery, I went through the painstaking rigmarole of joining Facebook. Then I turned to Larry and asked, "Now what do I do?" But on the day of the decision, I learned its value. Miriam's friends, from grade school through college, flooded our Facebook pages, expressing their outrage. Other friends showered us with letters and cards, filled with joyful memories of their times together.

AUGUST 21, 2009 was indeed a dark day for anyone believing in justice, either legal or biblical. Megrahi's "compassionate" release was based on a diagnosis that he suffered from prostate cancer and had only three months to live. That prediction turned out to be a farce.

"It's Embarrassing He's Lived So Long." This was the headline of a *London Sunday Times* article in July 2010, nearly a year later, saying:

> . . . The Libyan authorities seemed determined to find a doctor who would provide the three-month prognosis. Early efforts at the start of last year proved unsuccessful. Dr Stephen Harland, a consultant oncologist at University College London hospital, and David Dearnaley, professor of uro-oncology at the Royal Marsden hospital in London, both told the Libyans that Megrahi's lifespan was closer to nineteen months. Libya's ambassador to London subsequently turned to Professor Karol Sikora, medical director of Cancer Partners U.K. and dean of the medical school at Buckingham University. Sikora, who was paid £200 an hour for his services, said: 'It was clear that three months

was what they were aiming for. Three months was the critical point. On the balance of probabilities, I felt I could sort of justify [that].' Sikora now admits there was always a chance that Megrahi could live for much longer—possibly ten or even twenty years....

PROSTATE cancer is a disease that many elderly males experience and continue to live with for years. As Megrahi boarded a private Libyan jet, why were his face and head covered? Was it shame? Hardly. He has never uttered one word of remorse. Was it his debilitating condition? Ironically, when he disembarked in Tripoli, his face was uncovered and he wore a business suit, white shirt and bright red tie.

Dr. James Mohler, a prostate cancer expert at the Roswell Park Cancer Institute, stated: "There is no conceivable way that a cancer specialist or anyone familiar with the treatment of prostate cancer could have given Mr. Megrahi a three-month survival prognosis."

President Barack Obama had demanded that Libya keep Megrahi's return home low-key and not make a celebration of it. Gadhafi thumbed his nose. Thousands crowded the airport to greet the bomber as a hero. Frank Duggan told a reporter: "We knew there would be a hero's welcome for this murderous, wicked little man, and that is exactly what happened. It was obscene."

Why was this pariah allowed to go free? Why was the decision for his release made by one Scottish government minister and not by the Scottish court system? On August 22, 2009, the world learned the ugly truth. U.K. business deals with Libya had triggered this travesty just as *The Scotsman.com* had predicted. British Prime Minister Gordon Brown's own ministers admitted it. The *New York Times.com* reported:

"....Lord Trefgarne, chairman of the Libyan British Business Council, said Mr. Megrahi's release had opened the way for Britain's leading oil companies to pursue multi-billion-dollar oil contracts with Libya, which had demanded Mr. Megrahi's return in talks with British officials and business executives."

GADHAFI'S SON Saif revealed that the Prisoner Transfer Agreement was always on the table as part of trade negotiations with the U.K. Even worse, Megrahi wasn't transferred to a Libyan prison. Oh, no. MacAskill went the Libyans one better. He gave the bomber his freedom to return to the embrace of his family in Tripoli.

MacAskill said his decision would prohibit Megrahi from dying as a terrorist martyr. Larry and I asked: Then why not let the prisoner rot and die in prison in utter obscurity?

This justice minister also said, "Our beliefs dictate that justice be served but mercy be shown." What kind of ludicrous reasoning was that? For those of you who would turn the other cheek, there are not enough cheeks in the universe to measure up to the evil this man caused. A cheek is turned for a slap in the face. But there should not be a cheek receptive to a mass murderer of innocents. Mercy belongs to the remorseful and the repentant. Megrahi does not fit those descriptions. The Scots are just as angry as we are. Eighty percent of Americans polled believe the decision was a grievous miscarriage of justice perpetrated on all victims of terrorism. It was like handing a Get-Out-of-Jail-Free card to terrorists everywhere.

In January 2010 the earthquake fissure grew even wider as its jaws spit out the most damning revelations of all. Nile Gardiner, a Washington-based foreign affairs analyst, documented two disturbing facts: First, Megrahi participated in Libya's purchase and development of chemical weapons. Second, at the time of his release he had a Swiss bank account containing £1.8 million. Mr. Gardiner concluded that Megrahi was "a commanding figure in Tripoli's campaign of terror." Conservative Member of Parliament Ben Wallace, who is a member of the Scottish affairs committee investigating his release, said, "This suggests that Megrahi was an international coordinator of terrorism for Libya."

Did the Obama Administration do enough to oppose the

release? Some family members voiced skepticism. Frank Duggan vigorously responded: "The Administration efforts did not occur at the eleventh hour. Quite the opposite. . . .The Administration's opposition began over a year before the decision to free Megrahi, starting with the effort to hold the Brits' feet to the fire and not include Megrahi in the Prisoner Transfer Agreement."

Adding fuel to the fire was BP, the British Petroleum company. In April 2010 its Deepwater Horizon rig in the Gulf of Mexico exploded, spilling millions of gallons of crude oil—causing incalculable pollution, killing wildlife and destroying untold livelihoods.

In the wake of this disaster, a new exposé of BP came to light in mid-July 2010, dredging up fresh pain for the Pan Am families. In 2007, BP was working on a $900 million oil-and-gas exploration deal with Libya, but negotiations stalled. Jack Straw, British minister of justice at the time, has admitted that the lucrative BP deal was a consideration in deciding whether Megrahi should be released.

WUSA-Channel 9 in Washington, D.C. asked Frank Duggan if he thought the allegations against BP were true. "It's an oil company," said Frank. "Oil companies don't have souls. They make money. They make deals. Major corporations have always historically gotten involved in public policy issues affecting their bottom line."

The U.S. Senate held hearings. Scottish and British officials refused to attend. Chairman (of the hearings) Robert Menendez of New Jersey said: "The release on compassionate grounds was deeply, deeply flawed and perhaps even intentionally skewed to allow for al-Megrahi's release."

The idea of concluding this chapter on a bitter note disturbs me. So I won't. This is a fitting place to once again sing the praises of the Pan Am families group, those who do the daily, weekly, monthly and year-after-year work of representing us with their diplomacy, political skills, organizational expertise and compassion.

Here's an example. Gadhafi was scheduled to speak before the United Nations, shortly after Megrahi's release. Gadhafi planned to pitch his air-conditioned luxury tent in New Jersey, next door to the Libyan ambassador's estate. What chutzpah! Rubbing salt in our wounds. Thirty-three New Jersey residents died on Pan Am 103! The families' strong opposition forced him to go elsewhere. They then staged a massive demonstration in New York City—joined by other groups—on the day of Gadhafi's speech.

John O. Brennan, Assistant to the President for Homeland Security and Counterterrorism, spoke eloquently at the Pan Am Flight 103 Memorial Service at Arlington National Cemetery on December 21, 2009. In brief, he said:

> You—the families and friends of Pan Am Flight 103— have left a legacy all your own. You taught us that families can turn their grief into action and become powerful voices for change. For stronger security that protects our citizens. For legislation that ensures families are compensated. For sanctions that hold state sponsors of terrorism accountable for their crimes. And in so doing, you have inspired others touched by tragedy, including our 9/11 families.

EARLY IN 2011, a rising tide against oppression surged throughout North Africa and the Middle East. Uprisings against repressive governments in Tunisia, Egypt, Bahrain, and other countries spread to Libya. Gadhafi once again is showing his true colors. He is taking the hard line, using militia and mercenaries to ruthlessly quell the protestors. As of this writing, anarchy, violence and devastation rule the country.

CHAPTER 16

Letting Go—or Not

A YEAR AFTER THE TRIAL, I found a foot-high stack of sheet music on a bottom bookshelf in Miriam's room. When I say "found," I lie. I knew the stack was there. I just didn't want to deal with it. All her audition songs, all the music she hoped to sing on stage. That year one of the Miriam Wolfe scholarships at Temple Beth Shalom went to a high school senior who planned to major in musical theater at college. It was during a school day when I called her mother and offered her the music. The mother arrived at our house in thirty minutes. We barely spoke, she as choked with emotion as I. Standing in the doorway, I handed her the songs Miriam would never get to sing again.

Her upright piano stood against a wall in our living room, idle and out of tune. Neither Larry nor I played. As a kid, I had taken six years of totally wasted lessons. Hoping to present Larry with a special birthday gift, I practiced "The Flowers That Bloom in the Spring" from *The Mikado*, his favorite operetta. But when I played it for him, he didn't recognize it! The piano had been a gift from my father when Miriam was nine. The bench lid barely closed, so filled was it with her history. Crammed inside were all her piano lesson books; a plastic recorder; twenty-four playbills of shows and concerts she'd attended; an iron-on decal, "Blessed Are the Peacemakers"; a scissors with broken tip; her junior high band music; a newspaper article on "Parody, A Dying Art." Seventy-one items in all. I couldn't bear to throw any of them out—not for eighteen years. Larry and I finally gave away the piano, bench and lesson books. We made it a sentimental gift to Sara, a friend of Miriam's whose six-year-old daughter is already playing quite well. The sentiment ripples over three generations. Sara's mother, Sheila Litzky, introduced Larry to me. We're in our twenty-third year of marriage.

The playbills and stuff? Letting them go squeezed my heart dry, but I recycled them.

One of the boxes returned to us by the Scottish police contained the Oxford University sweatshirt Miriam had bought on a sightseeing trip. It's navy blue with a white emblem and Old English font. I have no idea whether she bought it for herself or for me. No matter. I immediately started wearing it and still do; it's comfy and fits me perfectly. During our first retirement winter in Honolulu, on an unusually cool morning, I wore it to play tennis with Larry. But soon I got overheated and tossed it on a bench. An hour later, as we were leaving, a foursome of Japanese men took over our court. We drove to our daughter Jackie's and as we pulled into the driveway, I shrieked, "Oh, no! I left my sweatshirt!" Larry turned the car around and back we went to the courts. As I opened the car door, one of the men left his game, picked the sweatshirt up off the bench and brought it to me. What an act of kindness. Somehow he knew it was mine and what it meant to me.

There's a lime green rug in Miriam's room, which is now a guest room. We bought the rug at Bill's Carpet Barn when she was fourteen. It goes with the wild rabbits romping through the grass on one wall. They're still happy and robust and refuse to leave. Fine with me. The rug was low-budget and so thin that we could cut it with a scissors. Down on our knees, we trimmed it to size to achieve the wall-to-wall effect. So why haven't I replaced it? Partly because I'm the world's laziest redecorator. And partly because— well, you know why. But when I do, it'll be the same lime green.

The FBI agent kept his promise and returned the jar of strawberry jam Miriam had made for my birthday. It sat in our pantry for twenty years with its calico ruffled cover, tied with red yarn. In 2008 I finally opened it. It was spoiled, thick with fuzzy mold. So why had I stubbornly saved it? What good did it serve?

There's more to the story of the Swatch watch that Miriam was wearing on the airplane home—my father's gift on her twentieth birthday. I had hid it away in a drawer. But on the day Father died, February 19, 1991, I started wearing it. I decided it brought me closer to them both. I wore it every day for thirteen years. Twice it needed a new band, but for the second one, a mall watch vendor bent the plastic brackets to accommodate it. Now I needed a third band, but nothing would fit the skewed brackets. I fussed, exasperated, visiting one jeweler after another, and even contemplated sending it to Swatch headquarters in Switzerland. But I needed a watch! I bought a Timex and gently laid the Swatch to rest in my safe deposit box. Time to let go.

Cardboard cartons in a corner of the guest room closet, five feet high, are filled with Miriam's original writings, art work from grade school, her report cards, snapshots and whatever. I cling to them. If I live to be 105, they'll still be there.

I only recently learned that the National Council of Jewish Women, Annapolis chapter, distributes gently used children's books. I'd already given some of Miriam's away, but we still had a full shelf in the basement. I scrubbed a tall stack of the most presentable ones and now they're making kids happy at the Boys and Girls Clubs and Head Start. The rest will go to whichever charity calls first, one that fixes and restores things. How did I not notice that my three-year-old was decorating some of her book covers with brown crayon?

I've talked about guilt, and how I've always worn it like a second skin. I'm better now, but not better enough. In a mall parking lot I'll see a mother hurrying to her car, her two small children trotting behind. She's not holding their hands, I notice. Tsk tsk. And then I silently scold myself: I'm judging her, but I didn't protect my own daughter on her way home from London. Totally illogical, I know; it was a group flight on a reputable airline, one

I myself had flown on. Occasionally, when I see a mother pushing her child in a stroller or shopping with her pre-teen, I want to start raising Miriam all over again. Next time, God, I'll do better. Such guilt is corrosive and destructive. Yet I allow it to mess with my head. But it's never too late to let go. On the TV show *Blue Bloods*, Detective Danny made a remark that I can apply to my guilt. "There's nothin' down that road. It's a dead end."

FOR LARRY and me, letting go means stepping over each new bad thing and moving on as best we can. Toughening our emotional hides.

There's an Italian restaurant in Annapolis I'll never set foot in again. It's not the restaurant's fault. It's what happened after we left it. On July 28, 2006, at ten o'clock at night, Larry and I said goodbye to our dinner companions. The six of us had started our evening at Temple Beth Shalom. Shabbat services always make me feel just a teeny bit righteous. But that night righteousness played no part.

Larry and I climbed into our minivan. He was driving, waiting for the green light to turn onto Route 2 for home. Suddenly he said:

"I can't breathe!"

He pulled onto the shoulder, we switched drivers and, thank heaven, Anne Arundel Medical Center was only five minutes away. But it was dark, I got disoriented, and Larry had to direct me to the hospital. In the Emergency Room, they took him immediately. He was having a heart attack. And to think that only two months earlier we'd been tramping around Japan.

As the interventionist-cardiologist prepared to install a stent, his associate came into the corridor where I sat—in inner panic. He explained what was going on and I scribbled everything he said in my little purse notebook. Then he asked me: "Do you have any questions?"

"Yes," I said, "but I don't know what they are."

The doctor understood and helped me out. "He's not going

to die. It's early."

Thank heaven again. The damage was minimal; within a year an EKG showed none at all. Nevertheless, for us a "small" heart attack is anything but. It's an unwelcome permanent guest, the gorilla in the living room.

But we don't obsess over it. In 2008 we sailed the Nile. For two years we taught a course on "Writing Mystery, Suspense and Thriller Fiction" at Anne Arundel Community College in Arnold, Maryland—offered in the Continuing Education Lifelong Learning Department. The second year we had seven students from the ages of, say, twenty-five to about seventy, all writing novels. Great stuff. We learned as much from them as they did from us.

The underlying thought that tugs at me every day is this: If Miriam were here, life would be perfect. In December 2008, a holiday letter arrived from Wendy Crouse, Miriam's best friend. As I knew, she had named her fourth child Miriam, born June 19, 2000. Wendy's words brought me as perfect a day as I'll ever have. She wrote:

I was at Temple Beth Shalom this past Saturday for one of my son Jacob's best friend's Bar Mitzvah. I think the last time I was inside the temple was at a service presenting the Miriam Luby Wolfe scholarship. As I was sitting at the service I realized that Jacob is within a year of the age I was when I met Miriam. It is such a strange thing to realize that Miriam and I really only met in eighth grade. It seems as though we were friends forever. I often look at my Miriam and think about how astoundingly like your Miriam she is—singing, dancing and bouncing everywhere she goes, even when she's just sharpening a pencil.

CHAPTER 17

Celebrations

Syracuse University Remembers

THE PLACE OF REMEMBRANCE—At the main entrance to Syracuse University, Larry and I huddled with other family members on the esplanade leading to the majestic Hall of Languages. We were gathered on April 22, 1990, for the dedication of the Place of Remembrance: a low granite and limestone wall inscribed with our thirty-five children's names. At the ceremony, Ronald Cavanagh, vice president for undergraduate studies, told us why the administration had chosen to situate the memorial at the very gateway to the school: "Not a place apart, obscure, or aloof and avoidable, but an undeniable, almost irresistible conduit of our collective energies, a place at the heart of our welcomes and farewells."

And so it is.

THE REMEMBRANCE SCHOLARSHIPS—That same year, SU created the annual Remembrance Scholarships Program. The thirty-five scholarships, worth $5,000 each, go to remarkable students for their senior year of study—each award designated to honor a particular student lost. The competition is keen; recipients are selected for their distinguished scholarship, citizenship and service to the community. Presentation takes place during the annual Remembrance Week: first at a Rose Laying Ceremony at the Wall and then at a convocation in Hendricks Chapel.

At the 2002 Convocation, Shazia Ashraf Bég spoke for all the Remembrance Scholars. She said:

> I come from Kashmir, a small valley in the Himalayas. Unfortunately, this beautiful land has become a battleground for its neighbors and as a result too many people have been killed, many of them innocent men, women and children. I myself have been a witness to a lot there, from being caught up in crossfire and barely making it out alive with my family to knowing someone or other who disappeared after being taken into custody.
>
> In one of the *Peanuts* cartoons Lucy reads a 'story' to her little brother, Linus. 'A man was born, lived and died.' Linus wondered: 'How fascinating. It makes you wish you knew the man.' As amusing as most *Peanuts* cartoons are for me, this particular one sent a different kind of message. As I read it, a chill ran down my spine thinking about the repercussions of being the person Lucy was describing. I knew I did not want to be like that man, someone without dreams, action or a purpose in life. Learning more and more about the Pan Am 103 and September 11th tragedies, and having experienced war firsthand myself, I know that I owe it to those victims to not remain naïve to other injustices happening in this world. We cannot let ourselves get entangled in the rat race of this world, engrossed in making more and having more—when there are those who live under oppression and without even the basics we take for granted. We may not be able to change the whole world, but the lives we have lost remind us that each one of us, in the little way we can, must try to do our share.

THE SYRACUSE-LOCKERBIE SCHOLARS—Another inspired annual program is the Syracuse-Lockerbie Scholarships, established at the Lockerbie Academy in Scotland, the area's regional high school. Two outstanding graduates receive scholarships to spend one year studying at SU. As one recipient's father said, that year "opened the world up" to his daughter and her entire family. SU Professor Christy Perry wrote in *Truth Quest* that the 2008-2009 scholars "were not even born when the plane exploded over their town. But they carry a legacy of peace and friendship as they leave their family, friends and alma mater to experience the university and New York and America. Syracuse University welcomes them."

THE PAN AM FLIGHT 103/LOCKERBIE AIR DISASTER AR-CHIVES—The PAF103 Archives contains a wealth of mementoes of our children, including a copy of *Miriam's Gift* and her published writings. It also contains records documenting the work of the families to promote justice, victims' rights and airline security. According to University Archivist Edward L. Galvin, "The archives has provided vital information for law enforcement, journalists, attorneys and victims' families." In 2006 the scope was expanded to include all 270 victims. Plans are under way to digitize much of the collection and make it available on the archives' web site.

THE PLAY'S THE THING—*The Women of Lockerbie*, a play by Deborah Brevoort, has been performed worldwide—but of most significance to me, in the Syracuse University drama department.

Written in the framework of a Greek tragedy, the play follows a grieving New Jersey mother to Lockerbie, where she searches the hills for any physical remains of her son, a passenger on Pan Am 103 whose body was never found. She encounters a chorus of townswomen. Angry, compassionate and determined, they seek to rescue the victims' clothes from the clutches of the U.S. State Department, whose envoy intends to have them burned. The drama reaches a catharsis when the Lockerbie women triumph—tenderly washing the bloodied garments in a stream, to be returned to the victims' families. This scene is a powerful interpretation of the facts in my chapter "Unexpected Gifts," where I describe the saintly people of Lockerbie.

In 2005, Larry and I received this letter from Kathryn Yohe:

Hello! I'm a senior acting major at SU and the Remembrance Scholar selected to represent Miriam this year. I first learned about Pan Am 103 in depth when I was cast in SU's drama production of *The Women of Lockerbie* last year. During our research period, your book, Ms. Mild, was absolutely invaluable and it became increasingly important to me as a person. The more I read excerpts of Miriam's journals, the more I am shocked by how much we have in common despite all the years that separate us. I, too, loved my semester in London. Wyeth's paintings are very important to me (I'm from his area of Pennsylvania) and I frequently refer to my copy of *The Tao of Pooh*. Miriam's a friend I wish I had. I've learned a lot about love and the value of life from learning her story (and yours). I consider it an enormous honor to represent your beautiful and talented daughter. I hope that both of you will be able to attend part of Remembrance Week so we can meet in person. Hopefully, you'll be able to see a performance of *A Remarkable Story*. Miriam's words are prominent throughout the show.

A Remarkable Story: The Voices Of Pan Am 103 was written by Joan Hart Willard, SU Assistant Professor of Drama. It premiered in August 2005 at the internationally renowned Edinburgh Fringe Festival. SU's Pan Am 103 Archives served as a wellspring of material for Joan: our kids' letters, journals, postcards, poetry, artwork—jubilant, funny and sometimes eerily prophetic. "The focus of our new production," she said in a letter to Larry and me, "is on the voices of the people who lost their lives on that terrible day; their words that were lost and then found and now heard. This story must be told again and again."

Nine drama students played as many as half a dozen roles, vividly capturing the personalities of the lost students—plus the viewpoints of embassy officials, an air traffic controller and a journalist. Kathryn played Theo Cohen. Heather Robb played Miriam. Joan e-mailed us this report after the performances:

> Miriam really made this play special; her beautiful prose gave the story a poetic soul. We opened the play with her letter to the Department of Programs Abroad, including her first letter home from London, describing her classes and how thrilled she was to be there; her letter describing her trip to Amsterdam and the Anne Frank Museum; and then closed with her description of Wales. It was a riveting and inspiring finale, listening to her beautiful words and the impact they had on the audience. Thank you, Miriam!

The Bird and the Two-ton Weight is a play by Darcy Fowler. In January 2008, Larry and I received an invitation from her and her actor friend Heather Robb to attend a reading. Darcy and Heather were 2005 SU graduates in the Department of Visual and Performing Arts. The following is an excerpt from the invitation:

> When we were seniors and cast in *The Women of Lockerbie,* our eyes were opened to the story of Pan Am 103. That's when we began to venture into the Syracuse archives. The more we learned, the more our lives were changed. We read journals of students like ourselves, who were going through the same things we were at the time and asking themselves the same questions we had asked ourselves. They even mentioned the same teachers we knew so well.
>
> Now, as actors and writers in New York, we have taken the next step in sharing this story. *The Bird and the Two-ton Weight* juxtaposes two lives: the life of a young

woman in 2008 trying to find her way and save her family after the death of her mother; and the life of a young woman in 1988, during her semester abroad in London, before her death in the Pan Am 103 tragedy. It is the story of what happens when these two lives collide through the discovery of a journal. It is a story about hope and possibility. We have been working on this play for a year now and it has met with overwhelming success. We are now in the process of turning the piece into a movie.

As luck would have it, Larry and I never got to attend any of these performances. We were either in Hawaii for the winter or Larry was recovering from back surgery. Darcy's reading took place at Lubin House, SU's New York City headquarters. Lubin House, a handsome brownstone in the East Sixties, was where Miriam auditioned as a high school senior for admission to the drama department. We went up on the train for the day. She came out of the audition room with the posture and sparkle of a singer who knows she's done well. In just those few hours, she met another applicant, a girl from Long Island, and they decided to room together (assuming correctly that they'd both get in). During the summer, Melanie even spent a week with us in Severna Park.

COMFORT IN CLOTH: THE SYRACUSE UNIVERSITY REMEMBRANCE QUILT—This insightful article was written by Dee Britton, Ph.D. and first published in *Voices*, the membership magazine of the New York Folklore Society (Vol. 34, Fall/Winter 2008). I have excerpted it here, with permission. Dr. Britton is an Assistant Professor of Social Sciences at the State University of New York's Empire State College.

On the evening of December 21, 1988, three thousand miles from the flames and wreckage of Lockerbie, Syracuse University faced its own devastation. Although many colleges and universities lost students as a result of the bombing of Pan Am 103, Syracuse University's loss of thirty-four undergraduates and one graduate student was one of the largest simultaneous student death tolls in United States' collegiate history. On the evening of the disaster, students, faculty and staff joined in a candlelight vigil. Over subsequent years, the university has held memorial services, constructed a Place of Remembrance and instituted a Remembrance Scholars program.

Collegiate traditions and rituals provide a group identity that transcends normal temporal boundaries. Yet colleges and universities are transitory in nature; students flow into and out of the university community as they matriculate and then graduate. Although the bombing of Pan Am 103 was a defining event for the school, it was "history" nearly ten years later to undergraduates who were between the ages of eight and twelve when the disaster occurred.

In 1998, the Remembrance Scholars gathered to discuss potential commemorative activities for the upcoming tenth anniversary. One of the scholars convinced her peers to create a remembrance quilt. There are many types of quilts, including patchwork, crazy, mourning, victory and friendship quilts. Historically, quilting has provided a sense of social solidarity and group identity. Remembrance quilts began to appear in the United States in the early 1800s. Individual blocks were made by the women of a community and were joined to create a quilt for someone who was leaving the community. In essence, the remembrance quilt was to remind the owner to remember those left behind as a result of a life transition.

The remembrance quilt concept was transformed by the NAMES Project's AIDS Memorial Quilt in 1987. The three-by-six-foot panels have been made by friends, family members, lovers and strangers. Some AIDS patients even created their own panels. The AIDS quilt currently comprises more than 46,000 panels.

The Syracuse community gathered together to quilt individual blocks to remind themselves of those students lost from the community. In a letter dated September 14, 1998, Remembrance Scholar Kimberly Hamilton described the quilt project to the parents of the Syracuse victims and requested information such as a favorite color, special talent, or longtime hobby. "We would also encourage you to send any items, fabrics, or photographs you would like incorporated in the quilt. No suggestion is out of the realm of possibility."

None of the Remembrance Scholars had quilting experience; nor did they realize the immensity of the task they had assumed. The quilt was to be presented at the tenth anniversary memorial service that would be held a mere three months and one week from the date of the letter. "Had I not been naïve about quilting," Hamilton later recalled, "I might never have proposed the idea. It has taken much more work than I ever imagined and at times has been very emotional."

Boxes containing personal objects began to arrive on campus: single earrings from the wreckage, their matches never found; an intramural field hockey shirt recovered from the debris. A mother sent fabric she had purchased with her daughter in London; they had planned to use it in a quilt project when her daughter returned. Photos abounded. A mother sent a piece of wallpaper from her daughter's childhood bedroom. Pajamas, a favorite shirt, a dusty Boston Red Sox cap, a cassette tape of a song written for one of the victims—all of these items were entrusted by grieving families to be incorporated into the quilt.

The Syracuse University Remembrance Quilt is not only a memorial for the bereaved and the university community, but also a work of art created in an intensely cooperative art world of beginning and experienced quilters. The Remembrance Scholars approached two Syracuse University staff members who were longtime quilters, as well as a group of quilters that met in the university chapel. A flyer inviting students, faculty and staff was distributed throughout campus. Twenty-nine students (including three males), six staff members and a faculty member's spouse answered the initial call. Individual quilt blocks were designed using the information and artifacts sent by the victims' parents. Students and staff worked to sew and then quilt each individual block. One staff member wanted to place at least two stitches in every student's block. A janitor worked on a block representing a young man from his hometown. Ten women who were members of a local quilting guild volunteered to devote an entire December day to completing the quilting, although they had no direct relationship with Syracuse University and had not known any of the students lost on Pan Am Flight 103. Their participation was symbolic of the social cohesion that resulted from the loss of so many students and is typical of the quilting community.

Each block is about the size of a standard sheet of paper (8.5 by 11 inches). The quilt's finished size is 87 by 91 inches. A center panel, measuring 36 by 58 inches, is surrounded by thirty-six individual blocks. The design of the center panel is based on an illustration created in 1989 by art student Jonathan Hoefer. A dove of peace is formed by the names of the thirty-five students. The Remembrance Scholars approached a university staff member, an experienced quilter, to create the center panel. Initially, she was hesitant, reasoning: "This is a painful thing for all of us. I have grieved privately for the thirty-five students who were lost in that terrorist attack. One side of me shies away, saying, 'It's time to let it rest, it's history, why bring it up again?' And the other side of me understands that those families do not want their children to be forgotten.

What a tragic thing to have so many talented young lives so cruelly thrown away, and what agony those families have had to endure. This is too worthwhile to ignore and I can see they need a lot of help to pull this off. I just wish they had started last February, not in mid-October!"

The machine-appliquéd work took her more than eighty hours over twenty-four days.

The thirty-five blocks are individual commemorations of the students, arranged alphabetically by last name. Letters that family members sent in response to the quilting project are folded accordion style and sewn into light orange borders adjacent to the student's block. A local sewing store volunteered to embroider the students' names on the blue lattice beneath the blocks. The individual blocks are poignant reminders. A pocket of a favorite shirt holds a cassette tape. Favorite authors and quotations are interspersed with athletic logos, flowers, musical instruments and theatrical symbols. On the upper right-hand corner of the quilt, two blocks are intertwined by blue and red bandanas tied together. Eric and Jason Coker were twins. When they were small, their mother dressed Eric in blue and Jason in red in order to identify them at a distance. As college students, they donned blue and red bandanas while they worked for a landscape company.

The quilt's thirty-sixth block is an embroidered dedication, using words borrowed from the university's memorial wall: "This Remembrance Quilt is dedicated to the memory of the 35 students enrolled in Syracuse University's Division of International Programs Abroad who died with 235 others as the result of a plane crash December 21, 1988, caused by a terrorist bomb."

The dedication wording is not the only component borrowed from other memorials for the Pan Am 103 victims. Steve Berrell's and Karen Hunt's quilt blocks include quotations that are also found on their plaques at Lockerbie's Garden of Remembrance in Dryfesdale Cemetery. Wendy Lincoln's block includes the dancer's silhouette that marks the headstone in her hometown cemetery. Cindy Smith's block includes an angel representing the mahogany angel carved in her memory and used every year in her hometown crèche.

The quilt was completed in time for the tenth anniversary memorial service. Its usual home is Hendricks Chapel at SU, but it has traveled to a number of different sites. After an exhibition in Lockerbie in 2000, a local representative wrote the following in the remembrance book that accompanies the quilt: "Remember us when you see these blocks. During its three week stay with us the Remembrance Quilt has brought with it an enormous wealth of feelings, thoughts, information and love. The love contained within it is overwhelming and is tangible. We in Lockerbie wish to include our love into the quilt's embrace and so with our love we send it back to you."

The Syracuse University Remembrance Quilt celebrates the individual lives lost on that winter solstice evening. The comfort and warmth that the quilt provides to family members and the Syracuse University community is unmatched by the many other memorials that dot the United States and Scotland. As Shannon Davis's mother stated, ". . . My heart still aches for Shannon not being with us. But when I see the quilt, I understand something bigger than us is at work."

MY DAUGHTER'S block is in the lower right corner. The request from Kimberly Hamilton sent me virtually soaring in a hot air balloon. I felt like packing up and shipping Miriam's entire room to her because I had so much to share. Days later, I had calmed down enough to send her a two-page letter, plus these mementoes: Her photo that I used for the cover of *Miriam's Gift*—taken in London by her dear friend and flatmate, Jessica Genick. Her silver seagull pin—she had a passion for the Chesapeake Bay. One of her favorite earrings. And a photo of her with her stepbrother, Chris Spencer. Next to it, imprinted in the fabric of her block, is the last paragraph of her letter to Chris on how to apply to college: "No matter what, do what's best for you. Your parents will love you no matter what. And, of course, so will I. I am sooo proud of you."

What takes my breath away even today is not only the skill, but the love and tenderness revealed by the quilters. The Remembrance Scholars added other appropriate symbols. Those for my daughter included a stack of books; a musical staff; and the song title "Memory" from *Cats*, which she loved to sing. Before we attended *Cats* together at the National Theatre in Washington, D.C., Miriam and I read T.S. Eliot's *Book of Impossible Cats*, on which the show is based. We found it astonishing that the lyrics followed the poems almost word for word. And when the tattered Grizabella sang "Memory" we held hands and cried.

The Remembrance Quilt was on display at a hotel in Washington during a briefing for Pan Am families by then-Attorney General Janet Reno, who graciously spoke with all of us personally after the briefing. I presented her with a copy of *Miriam's Gift*. Later that day, family members saw her studying the quilt's individual blocks. (See "A Photo Album," which includes photos of the entire quilt and Miriam's block.)

Maryland Remembers

IN OUR joyful corner of Maryland, remarkable young men and women have received awards established in Miriam's memory.

TEMPLE BETH SHALOM—At Temple Beth Shalom in Arnold, the Miriam Luby Wolfe Scholarship Fund is open to students age thirteen to eighteen. The recipients are chosen for outstanding academic achievement, community involvement, participation in the arts and other activities, and a commitment to Jewish ideals and temple life. When the award originally went to elementary school kids as well, one winner was Laura, an eight-year-old who sang and danced. Her mother just happened to have performed in *The Music Man* with Miriam during the summer of 1986; she was pregnant with Laura at the time! The awards committee didn't know this, of course. Just an eerie coincidence. The award winners apply it in many ways. Michael spent his senior year of high school at New York University. Miriam was Paul's camp counselor; he used his scholarship toward tuition at the University of Pennsylvania, where he planned to minor in Judaic Studies. Rachel and Scott used their awards for a trip to Israel. Julie used hers to attend the summer Pre-College Music Theater Program at Carnegie Mellon University. Zane, a sophomore, was already multitasking "to make our temple community, my hometown, and the world better places." Paige, the 2011 winner, aspires to become a surgeon and hopes to use the award for a laptop computer for college.

SEVERNA PARK HIGH SCHOOL—At Severna Park High School, the English Department created the annual Miriam Luby Wolfe Memorial English Award. I present it at the senior awards ceremony. The recipients have touched my heart with their excellence. Among them are a poet and a Shakespeare scholar.

I'm always invited to give my own brief spiel at this ceremony, where I present an autographed copy of *Miriam's Gift,* a check and copies of Miriam's published writings. I'm so grateful to be invited; I wouldn't miss this opportunity for anything. And yet, these moments are bittersweet. At Severna Park High, speaking before hundreds of parents and seniors, I sometimes hear my voice shaking. Miriam herself was up on this very stage receiving awards with the class of 1986.

CHILDREN'S THEATRE OF ANNAPOLIS—Children's Theatre of Annapolis also presents scholarships in her memory to high school seniors who are deeply involved in CTA and intend to continue on in the performing arts. CTA has developed a really cool tradition. They treat all the CTA seniors to an evening at a dinner theater. It's always a delightfully raucous event, with my presentation taking place during the intermission of shows such as *Oklahoma* or *Aida* or *Little Shop of Horrors*.

In 2006 I received a large brown envelope from the Register of Wills in Annapolis. What could they possibly want with me? My fingers turned cold as I slit it open. It was a copy of the will of Bernardine "Dina" McPherson. Dina taught psychology at Severna Park High and became a good friend of Miriam's when they were both summer counselors at London Town colonial history camp. Dina had died much too young, of cancer. Her will contained a bequest to honor Miriam's memory: "$1,000 to Rosemary Mild, the mother of Miriam Wolfe, to be used by her for a scholarship fund. She shall have sole discretion of selecting the scholarship fund." I donated the check to CTA.

IT CAN BE gratifying to make a donation to a special cause in a loved one's memory because we're doing something tangible and lasting. Predictably, here are my favorites:

Miriam Luby Wolfe Scholarship Award
Temple Beth Shalom
1461 Baltimore-Annapolis Boulevard
Arnold, Maryland 21012

Miriam Luby Wolfe Memorial Scholarship
Children's Theatre of Annapolis
P.O. Box 1785
Annapolis, Maryland 21404

Remembrance Scholarship Endowment Fund
Syracuse University, Office of Development
820 Comstock Avenue
Syracuse, NY 13244-5040
http://secure.syr.edu/giving/default.aspx

And whenever any of my favorite charities include a line for "in memory of" I put in Miriam's name.

Other Families Remember

MANY OTHER Pan Am 103 families have created memorials that reflect the specialized interests and passions of their lost loved ones. Among them:

- A baseball field for disabled children.
- A Little League field to be used by the Challenger Division.
- A scholarship for a science degree.
- A cabin for use by the Dartmouth College Outing Club.
- A golf outing to benefit a University of Dayton scholarship.
- A painting illustrating a poem written by a lost friend.
- Scholarships for high school graduates from the South Bronx.
- An annual art show to benefit young artists.
- Development of a music rehearsal hall at a university.

Sculptor Suse Lowenstein, mother of SU student Alexander Lowenstein, created *Dark Elegy*, a grouping of seventy-five larger-than-life-size sculptures of mothers (including herself), wives and grandmothers who lost loved ones on the plane—with each woman posed at the moment when she learned the terrible news. Negotiations are currently under way for a permanent, prominent location for *Dark Elegy*.

CHAPTER 18

To Blossom Again and Again and Again

In the depth of winter, I finally learned that within me
there lay an invincible summer.—Albert Camus

WHEN TWA FLIGHT 800 exploded in 1996 in a fireball off Long Island, I could not watch the news reports. For two days I was in a state of denial. My chest was tight, my throat was constricted. I felt like I was choking. Over and over on TV, I saw the shots of Pan Am Flight 103 lying in the Scottish countryside, a broken, dead beast. And I was being dragged back nearly eight years to relive my own horror.

My heart ached for those families. So many children on board. Losing a child is the ultimate hell. There is no getting over it. So much love, so much potential destroyed. To this day, government officials and witnesses disagree on what caused TWA 800 to explode, but I knew what lay ahead for those TWA families. The moment Miriam died I became an unwilling public figure. We all did, all of us who waited that night beside phones and in airports for our loved ones who would never come home.

The night after my daughter died, I woke up screaming from a bone-chilling nightmare. In the dream, I was huddled with my grieving family at her graveside as we were burying her. Suddenly, a sinister band of men, wearing camouflage uniforms and carrying machine guns, poured out of a bus and came thundering toward us. It was a terrifying image. For nearly five years, I had these grotesque dreams that wouldn't let me rest.

My nightmares were not confined to the night. A generalized anxiety, a foreboding lurks inside me still, hovers over me, shadows me throughout my day. Will the terrorists plant a bomb on the next plane I travel on? Or will it happen on the Metro as I benignly head for the National Gallery of Art in Washington, D.C.?

Even worse is the daily nightmare of living without Miriam. Not having her to talk to. I hear Bette Midler sing "The Rose" on the radio; I have a tape of Miriam singing "The Rose," so sweetly, so exquisitely it makes me cry. I can no longer tolerate one of my favorite pieces of music, *Pomp and Circumstance*, because now its majestic motif represents the college graduation Miriam was denied.

My dreams aren't always nightmares. Miriam is often in my dreams—always alive and well, perky and exuberant, vigorously pursuing her daily life. And paired with this nighttime fantasy is an obsessive, irrational thought that keeps pressing against my skull: Okay, I've proved that I'm strong; I can handle suffering; I can function and be productive; I continue to nurture my husband and family. I've been tested and I passed. Now I want her back.

But it isn't going to happen, not in this life. So I content myself with the next best thing: perpetuating her legacy, which continues to surge like ocean waves on the world. Her charisma left indelible impressions. Four friends and a cousin have named their babies after her. After I published one of her short stories in *Cricket*, an eight-year-old from Minnesota wrote to say that in the year she'd had her subscription, Miriam's story was one of her two favorites.

In the corner of a drawer, I keep a small brown rock sent to me by a girl who lives on Prince Edward Island, Canada. She picked it up on the actual farm where *Anne of Green Gables* takes place. Miriam performed the comic role of Mrs. Spencer in the play. So my daughter's impact weaves through new lives, touching the hearts and souls of yet another generation.

Shortly after publication in 1999, I sent a copy of *Miriam's Gift* to President Bill Clinton. He wrote me this: "Thank you for your kind letter and the copy of your book. Your courage and your dedication to preserving the memory of your daughter are a testament to the strength of the human spirit. Hillary and I are touched that you shared this special tribute with us. We send our best wishes to you and Larry."

I often wonder—what would my beloved daughter be doing if she were still here? She'd have graduated from Syracuse in 1990. She'd be performing—singing, dancing, acting.

She'd be directing plays. Perhaps she would have even started her own theater company by now (she was already studying grantsmanship). She planned to write, direct and produce; do tours, workshops, political issue theater. She'd be teaching acting to children. She'd be writing plays and poems. Maybe she'd be a professional writer—or blogging her way into fame. In London she made a list of "Things I Really Want to Do: Become a therapist some day. Work in a drug/alcohol rehab center. Teach high school kids and work with toddlers. Study government and politics." Most likely she'd be doing a fair share of all these things by now.

What else might Miriam be doing? She'd be living in an apartment in New York or Chicago. She'd be visiting Larry and me, playing Big Boggle with us—and winning. She'd be hugging me, laying her head on my shoulder, or wanting me to hear "just this one song" or "just this poem" even though it's midnight. She'd be debating with Larry or rolling her eyes at one of his puns. I would hope she'd be contentedly married—and a mother by now.

We received a few condolence notes saying the blowing up of Pan Am 103 was "God's will" and "Everything happens for a reason." Some people need to believe that for their own peace of mind. I don't believe it for a minute. The very idea strikes me as not only outrageous, but blasphemous, an injustice to God.

Nevertheless, I have raged in my private moments, asking myself the age-old questions. How could a good, just and loving God have let this happen? At first, engulfed in self-pity, I cried,

"Why me?" And then, after much deliberation, I saw the question as "Why them?" There were babies on that plane and more than a hundred passengers in their twenties. Can it be God's will to put such a loving, gifted creature as Miriam on this earth and then take her away before she has reached her full potential?

The night Miriam died, for a fleeting moment I told myself there is no God. But I immediately squashed that thought—mostly in fear that if I persisted in voicing it, I would bring even greater devastation down on myself. In succeeding days, the heretical thought revisited me, refusing to go away; it festered and infected my logical thinking. Again I asked myself: Could He be a just and loving God if He allowed a Pan Am 103 to happen? Is there a God at all? And what has become of life's natural rhythm and the harmony of His heavenly universe?

I'm a stubborn person. Letting go was hard enough when it meant Miriam's playbills and piano. But anger is another matter entirely. How do I let go of anger when evil is rewarded? And should I let go? The bomber of our 270 loved ones was set free and returned home to his family in Libya. Other cases of unfathomable injustice, laid end to end, would encircle our planet many times over. So today I wrestle with a different perspective. Evil exists because God gave us free will. But did He have to give us so much of it?

I already know the answer. The universe was not created with a flawed blueprint. It's the terrible wrongs that evil men contrive to disrupt His glorious plan for a harmonious existence. There must be a God, because He gave me Larry—and Jackie and Myrna and Rodney and Tim and our grandchildren. Alena was born the week of Miriam's twentieth birthday. Craig, five weeks old, slept in Myrna's arms in our living room as we sat *shivah*. And then along came our precious Ben, Leah and Emily.

Now our grandchildren range in ages from thirteen to twenty-two. Ben, a champion competitive rider, juggles college classes with training quarter horses on the family farm. Craig traveled to Fiji for his graduate field work in anthropology. In his rakish khaki hat (which his brother, Ben, bought him), cargo shorts, backpack and boots, he looked like Indiana Jones himself. Alena graduated from the University of Washington with majors in art and psychology. Leah sent us her well-reasoned compositions from the University of San Francisco; one documented the importance of art and music in elementary and high schools. When Emily isn't in middle school, she plays sports and volunteers at an SPCA. A week after her last visit to us in Severna Park, I discovered a mysterious cardboard box, tied with red ribbon, on one of our office shelves. Inside were drawings of me that Emily had done in ballpoint pen on a yellow legal pad.

Among the hundreds of friends, family members and even the most remote acquaintances who came to our house, there wasn't one who wasn't thinking, Thank God Rosemary has Larry. So true. And God has been good to me in giving me all our cherished relatives and dear friends, who make up our extended family.

When your only child has been murdered, does grief include a lifetime of bitterness? It inflames me when I read about monster parents like a mother who deliberately drowned her two small sons. By what right, by what higher authority did that mother deserve her children when I, who was so loving and nurturing, have been deprived of mine? But that train of thought won't get me anywhere. Evil exists in the world; it's a fact of life. In *Mishkan T'filah*, our new Reform prayerbook, we pray: "May the time not be distant, O God, when all shall turn to you in love, when corruption and evil shall give way to integrity and goodness, when superstition shall no longer enslave the mind, nor idolatry blind the eye." Until such time, there will be evil in the world—and I tell myself that raging against monster parents and the injustice of it all is self-defeating.

On the High Holy Days, for years after Miriam's death, I sat in temple crying more than meditating, crying more than singing, crying more than praying. I was surrounded by Miriam's friends from religious school, Confirmation and Youth Group. I cried because they're here and she isn't. Many are married and have children. I read my prayer book. It tells us to forgive, forgive, forgive. But I can't forgive the terrorists. I never will.

The last few years I've cried a little less—because of one passage in the prayerbook. It speaks of God leading our people out of Egypt to serve Him in freedom. "Full of joy, Moses and Miriam and all Israel sang." Somehow, reading that passage, in the very tangible speaking of Miriam's name, I felt renewed.

In every service we recite the Kaddish, the mourners' prayer. The origins of the Kaddish are mysterious. According to *Gates of Prayer*, angels are said to have brought it down from heaven. The Kaddish never acknowledges death. Instead, it permits the blossom, which has fallen from the tree of humankind, to flower and grow again in the human heart. The Kaddish mentions neither death nor grief. Instead, it extols the glory of God. It represents a moral triumph for the mourner because the prayer turns attention away from our inwardness, away from our individual sorrow to focus on the glory of God and the hope for a better life for all. And I try to remember our Yom Kippur memorial book's words:

"We do our best homage to our dead when we live our lives most fully, even in the shadow of our loss. For each of our lives is worth the life of the whole world."

AT TEMPLE BETH SHALOM, Rabbi Ari Goldstein told us a story about the great violinist Yitzak Perlman—a man who contracted polio at the age of four and overcame his severe physical handicaps to share his gift with the world. During a major concert, Mr. Perlman began playing, when suddenly one of his violin strings broke. The conductor signaled the orchestra to stop. The packed house sat hushed. Everyone expected Mr. Perlman to ask for another violin or at least a new string. But he didn't. He motioned for the conductor to continue and played the entire concert minus the broken string. Afterward, he was asked why. Yitzak Perlman replied:

"We make music with what we have, and when that's gone, we must make music with what we have left."

Where will I find the music that will give me peace? Ten

years ago, I thought that maybe, just maybe, my fears and night-mares would end if the Libyan bombers were incarcerated for life. Even that prospect has dried up—in a desert of cynicism. If we in America ever felt protected by the oceans that surround us, that sense of security evaporated with the bombing of the Alfred P. Murrah Federal Building in Oklahoma City; the destruction of the World Trade Center; the murder of thirteen military personnel at Fort Hood, Texas; and the murder of a security guard at the U.S. Holocaust Memorial Museum in Washington, D.C. Terrorism, both foreign and home-grown, is now part of our local criminal landscape.

Have the terrorists defeated me personally? No—because I am Miriam's mother. She remains a part of my very soul. She nurtures me. Her memory blooms richly in all who knew her. No terrorist can destroy that. I will continue to perpetuate her joyful outlook, to find within me Camus' "invincible summer." Miriam herself was a crusader, she was determined to make the world a better place, but at the same time she had a passionate appreciation of God's gifts to us and an innocent confidence, as did Anne Frank, in the basic goodness of people.

An acid irony eats at me: I live in a world so imperfect that it took my daughter from me. Still, her optimism sustains me every hour of my life. In one of her journals, returned to me by the Scottish police, she kept an account of her exhilarating side trip to Wales. Sitting on a hillside at dusk, gazing at Kidwelly Castle, she wrote:

"The sky was bluer today, the sun was yellower today, and the whole of the earth seemed to be rejoicing in its own perfection!"

More of Miriam's Writings

<u>STORIES</u>

Outstanding in the Field

"DO YOU THINK we'll win?" I asked.

"Probably," Shannon answered. She sighed and cracked her Juicy Fruit, which must have been completely flavorless by now. After all, we'd been sitting on the bench for over two hours.

The baseball game was almost over. Only a few more minutes of being Green Hornets before Shannon and I could start being regular sixth graders again. Maybe my mom would take us to Baskin Robbins on the way home. I daydreamed about how wonderful the air-conditioned ice cream parlor would feel after a day like this.

Shannon nudged my arm and pointed to our coach, Mr. Lanahan. He was standing with the umpire and the other team's coach.

"I'm sure it was a ball. That's my final decision," the umpire said.

"Are you blind? That pitch was inside—an inside strike." Mr. Lanahan argued.

Mr. Lanahan always made a fuss over at least one call per game and it was usually a play involving his daughter, Carol Jane. Finally, he noticed how ineffective his arguing was and ended the time-out.

Carol Jane pitched the ball. The batter caught a piece of it and we watched Carol Jane jump to catch the pop-fly. With the ball safely in her glove, she fell gracefully to the ground and rolled over and over. Shannon and I remained unimpressed—Carol Jane always fell to the ground after she completed a difficult play. The fans, however, applauded wildly as her theatrical catch ended the game in our favor.

Mrs. Lanahan was grinning from ear to ear and gushing, "Oh, I'm so proud of you girls. Carol Jane, honey, drink some water—you must be exhausted. Sarah, that throw from home to second was fantastic! Come here, child, and let me hug you. Melanie, you're quite the little powerhouse. That triple will be a home run before long."

As annoying as she was, I wished that Mrs. Lanahan would give me a postgame hug—just once. I looked at Shannon, who seemed to be thinking the same thing.

Shannon and I stood in front of Mrs. Lanahan, waiting for some acknowledgment. When we received none, we shrugged at each other and with visions of Rocky Road ice cream and raspberry sherbet dancing in our heads, ran for the parking lot.

We were almost out of earshot when Mrs. Lanahan called to us. "Girls: Shannon and Miriam, Mr. Lanahan needs your attention for just a few minutes." We stopped in our tracks and walked slowly back.

"Well, girls," Mr. Lanahan was saying, "I cannot tell you how proud I am of each and every one of you. Now that we're in the play-off, we're going to have to practice harder than ever so we can go out and show 'em what real teamwork is. I want you to go home and rest up—you'll need plenty of energy for Tuesday's practice."

With Mr. Lanahan done, Shannon and I were anxious to flee. But this time, it was my mom who prevented us. She had sat through the entire game without seeing Shannon or me so much as grasp a bat.

She walked up to Mr. Lanahan and said pleasantly, "Hi, I'm Rosemary, Miriam's mother. I realize that today's game was an important one, but my daughter and Shannon didn't get to play at all. Miriam enrolled in baseball as a learning experience and I'd like her to have it."

Mr. Lanahan thought for a moment and then said, "Of course, Rosemary, I have every intention of playing her in the next game. I give you my word."

"Thank you," said my mother sweetly and she took us to the car.

Tuesday came and it was time for our big practice—the one to get us in shape for the play-off. Practice started out with fielding drills. As usual, Shannon and I sat on the bench to watch.

All of a sudden, Mr. Lanahan yelled to us, "Shannon, you take third base. Miriam, take second."

Shannon and I sat there wide-eyed. Apparently, he was willing to give us a chance.

We ran out to assume our positions. Mr. Lanahan started by hitting me a few grounders, which I threw too slowly to get the imaginary runner out at first. Then Mr. Lanahan hit some fly balls. I knew that I was supposed to hold my glove up in front of my face, but I couldn't bring myself to do it. Instead, I held the glove about waist high, as one would hold a cup and saucer. As a result, I dropped or missed every ball that came my way. Carol Jane shot me dirty looks through the entire practice. When it was over, Shannon and I set the new world's record for the fifty-yard dash from the field to the parking lot. Well, there were always thirty-one flavors to drown our sorrows in.

All week long, Shannon and I dreaded the Saturday play-off. At first, I'd been thrilled that my mother had taken my part, but the more I thought about it, the more I wished she hadn't. "Mom," I finally asked, "why did you have to go and talk to Mr. Lanahan?"

"I thought you wanted me to," she said, surprised. "You were coming home from practices all upset because you weren't being given a chance to play."

"Couldn't you have let me handle it myself?"

"Why are you so upset? On Saturday you seemed pleased that something was finally getting done."

"I was," I said. "But, I didn't think that would mean I'd actually be in the play-off."

"So that's what's bothering you," my mother said. "Miriam, just do your best and everything will be fine." She gave me a hug.

I wasn't so sure that everything would be fine. When Shannon and I left for the game on Saturday, my stomach was doing backflips and my heart was in my mouth.

We arrived at the field and practically fell over each other to get to our bench. Once there, we began to relax a little.

The first four innings went by quickly. We were winning 4-2 and neither Shannon nor I had been called to play. At the top of the fifth, however, Carol Jane dropped the ball after catching a fly and two players on the opposing team ran home. The score was now 4-4 and some of our girls were getting tired.

Suddenly, I heard Mr. Lanahan calling. "Miriam! I want you in right field. Shannon, take center field."

Shannon and I were scared to death, but we took our positions. I spent the next hour standing in the field, praying, "Please God, don't let any balls come out here."

Carol Jane was pitching well and our girls were doing a good job of fielding, so we managed to hold off any more runs until the bottom of the final inning. The score was 5-4 in our favor. The next player up to bat got two strikes and three balls. We were one strike away from winning the play-off.

Then it happened. The batter whacked Carol Jane's next pitch with tremendous force. The ball sailed over her head and right toward me, standing in right field. Of course, I didn't put the glove up to receive the ball, because I thought I'd get socked in the face. Holding my glove like a teacup and saucer, I extended my arm as the ball descended—and landed securely in my glove.

All the girls on my team were smiling at me as I stood there, frozen, holding the ball. Then they started yelling and motioning toward Carol Jane. It finally dawned on me that I was supposed to throw the ball back to her. We had won the championship.

The next thing I saw was Mrs. Lanahan running toward me across the field. She looked like a person in a movie, running to the sound of violins across a field of daisies. She reached me after what seemed an eternity.

"Oh, Miriam," she said, "I'm so proud of you." She stretched out her arms and gave me a huge hug. It was the moment I'd been waiting for. But as I stood there, smothered in her arms, suddenly all I could think about was a big dish of Rocky Road. Desperately, I looked over at Shannon. She understood and motioned toward the parking lot.

Tufts Luck

"A CHIPWICH and a Sunkist, please." I pay the Good Humor man and run to join David, Alice and Susan under our tree. We love eating lunch here because we feel so collegiate, arguing and working under our tree—just like the covers of the catalogues that now arrive daily in all our mailboxes. I put my book bag down first to avoid getting grass stains on my slacks.

"Have you heard anything yet?" I ask David.

"Sarah, I think you'd know if he had," Alice laughs. "When that day comes, no doubt the whole school will know."

"Only if the results are favorable," David says as he pinches Alice's thigh. She squeals and smacks his hand.

"Then I take it that you haven't heard anything either, Susan?"

"No, Sarah, I haven't heard from Tufts," Susan says as she points a finger at me. "But I did get offered a full scholarship to Slippery Stone U. or something like that."

"That's great, Susan!"

"Sarah, reserve judgment until you know the whole story. It's an institution to which I did not even apply. Sounds like a selective place, no?" Susan laughs and tosses her head back in an attempt to look casual. She fools no one. Even though it's early in the year, the pressure of applying to colleges is increasing daily—almost as quickly as the temperature outside is decreasing.

"Scored that high on your SATs, Susan?" David teases.

"I wouldn't laugh if I were you," Susan warns. "Especially

considering the fact that you and I have identical GPAs and SAT scores!"

"Just where is this Slippery Boulder place, anyway?" David never knows when to stop.

"Slippery Rock." Alice eases the tension, as usual. "You're both wrong. It's Slippery Rock U. And, anyway, why is it, David, that you can't conceive of a school in anyplace but Boston?"

David is preparing a rebuttal long before Alice finishes her sentence.

"You laugh," he says, "but no other place in the East equals it; the shopping is just incredible, and you can't beat it culturally."

"Well," says Susan, "I hope we do both end up in Boston, but not everyone thinks of shopping opportunities first and foremost when looking at schools."

"I agree with Susan," I pipe in. "I'm just grateful that I've got another year to wait. I've got to narrow my list of schools down."

"I still think you should go to Bennington for drama, Sarah."

"David, that school is just 600 women living in Vermont. What do I want with 600 women in Vermont? It's also the second most expensive school in the country."

"So take out a loan." David still doesn't get it.

"Even with loans, David, I CAN'T AFFORD IT!" I'm getting angrier by the minute and start to say things I probably shouldn't. "I know that the concept of no money is hard for someone like you to understand. But, MY grandfather didn't fund an entire new library wing at MY first choice school! You're luckier than most people."

The bell rings. Time to go back to class. I'm saved, literally, by the bell. David and Susan walk off together and Alice and I follow behind them.

"I'm so sick of David's baloney," I say to Alice. "I used to buy into everything he said. I spent months thinking that I'd be a failure in life if I went anywhere but an Ivy League school. But then I came to my senses. I'm worried about Susan. She's putting too much stock in getting accepted to Tufts."

"I know," Alice says, "But look at David—he'll be devastated if he doesn't get in."

"But he will, Alice. He's third generation there, for God's sake!"

"I don't know, Sarah, it's an awfully selective place."

I nod. There's nothing more to do but wait and see.

January 12. DEFERRED. I didn't even know what that meant until today. But that's what both Susan and David got from Tufts. This means, basically, that Tufts wants to stall on making a decision about them. Fine. As long as they're both still in the running.

We're in the cafeteria now. It's too cold to eat outside. The walls are prison gray.

"I really screwed myself up," David is saying as he sits down to eat. I ask him why.

"Because I should have applied as a history major, instead of pre-law."

Again I ask why.

"Because history is an easier major to get into at Tufts. It's less competitive."

"But that means you'd be lying, wouldn't it? If you plan to major in pre-law, wouldn't you be putting yourself in a bind if you said you were interested in history? I guess I'm naive."

"No. Everyone does it, it's a common practice. Just like lying on your transcript."

"Just like what?" I can't believe my ears.

"Like lying on a transcript. You know, like putting down activities that you were never involved in. It's easy to do—they never check the facts."

"Terrific, David. Just terrific." Disgusted, I leave the group in search of some freshmen friends who don't know or care that Tufts is in Boston.

March 15. REJECTION. Susan has been rejected. Tufts, her dream school, turned her down. She's not taking it too well.

"I'd beg and plead if I thought it would help," Susan is telling me. I'm surprised to hear words like this come out of her mouth.

David is also devastated—he too was rejected. It looks as if he will not carry on the family tradition of graduating from Tufts. I'm angry. The Admissions Office called David's grandfather personally to apologize for David's being rejected. Susan got a form letter.

March 20. "You'll never guess what happened to me," David says as he runs up to me.

"Don't make me guess."

"I got an acceptance letter from Tufts in the mail yesterday!"

"But that's impossible. What happened?" David, thinking my question rhetorical, turns and heads for the soda machine.

Once he is out of earshot, Susan asks, "What the hell is going on?"

Alice tells her, "Someone in Admissions realized that David's family has made a rather large investment in their school and I guess they decided not to jeopardize it."

"I'm sickened," Susan says. I don't blame her.

I hesitate as I approach our tree, where Alice and David are already eating. David is lying on his side, with his elbow propping him up. I half expect Alice to be fanning him and feeding him grapes. The weather's balmy, but there's a breeze. I hear a loud rumble. Thunder. A squall is building. The wind blows my skirt up. I sit down quickly, embarrassed.

"Doing your Marilyn Monroe impression for us today, Sarah?" David's sky-blue eyes sparkle mischievously. I'd hit him if he weren't so damned cute.

But I know how to get to him—he prides himself on being socially adept. "Watch it, David. If you were really a gentleman, you'd have pretended not to notice!"

"You know that I could never pass up a chance to comment on those gorgeous legs of yours," David says.

"Flattery will get you everywhere," I say and smile at him.

"You should try some of this flattery stuff with me—I think I'd like it, in time!" Alice says to David, smiling a bit tensely. She cannot, no matter how hard she tries, get used to her boyfriend flirting with other girls, even when they're good friends like me who aren't even interested! Susan walks up. Her book bag makes a loud thud as it hits the ground. She's about to explode with rage. A funny feeling in my stomach tells me that I'll know why before lunch ends. Another rumble of thunder. Two storms are approaching simultaneously.

"So, David," Susan says with an edge to her tone, "have you sent in your Tufts housing deposit yet?" She puts a mockingly God-fearing tone into the words "Tufts housing deposit."

"That sounds more like an accusation than a question," David says, sitting up.

"Well," says Susan, "I've heard every other little tidbit about Tufts from everyone but you, so I wondered what the latest is. Aren't there any little facts you'd like to share with me? Things you might've left out when speaking to the masses?"

"Susan, you're overreacting. I told a couple of people some things the day I got in, because I was so excited."

"A couple of people, David? Don't make me laugh!"

"All right, all right . . . five people at the most." David winks at me, trying to include me in what he sees as just a little tiff over nothing. I ignore his mugging—I can see that this means an awful lot to Susan. Alice and I look at each other and she suggests with a nod that we retreat so that David and Susan can argue privately. We move to a bench where we should be out of earshot, but we can still hear everything clearly.

"What do you want from me?" David is practically yelling now. "Do you expect me not to go to Tufts in protest of your rejection?"

"Don't be an idiot. Of course that's not what I want. I just thought you'd be a little smarter than to go to a school that only accepted you because of your economic status."

"You little bitch. You're so jealous you don't know what to do. That's fine—I'd be jealous too. But don't you go pinning all your resentment on me. I won this war, that's all. I just thought you'd be a better sport."

"That's it—I don't think I can take any more, I'm getting nauseated."

Susan gets up. Even from where I'm sitting, I can see the tears welling up in her eyes. She'll never cry in front of him, though. She's too strong for that. I can't believe this is happening now. After all we've been through together. Right before their graduation.

David's really out of hand. I never knew he thought of it as a war. I'm learning more about him than I really want to know.

A crash of thunder and the drops start to hit us. This rain is hard and cold and coming down fast. I'm soaked before I even get to my book bag. Just like this storm, I've expected this fight for a long time. Somehow, though, it's a shock when it happens. We won't all be friends forever. It's hard to know who you can trust. Like the rain that hits me cold and hard, something else hits me: reality.

Summer Job Blues

THERE IS NO summer job more nerve-wracking than playing camp counselor to a pack of rug-rats. This was my belief as I tried to put fifty screaming children on their respective buses home.

There were four buses, each designated by color. So, I called the kids on the Red Route and had them stand to one side, and did the same for the Green, Yellow and Blue routes. To my astonishment, the kids cooperated. Every kid got into his bus group— that is, every kid except one: Warner Chase. I'll never forget that name.

Warner stood alone under the oak tree, guiltily picking his freckled nose. This didn't phase me because Warner often stood around with his finger in his nostril. At a distance, he looked deceptively angelic; he was a small child with light brown hair, freckles and hazel eyes. But I knew Warner Chase and was not about to be fooled. I eyed him resentfully and spoke in my "Mommie Dearest" voice.

"Warner, are you riding a bus today?"

"I dunno."

"You don't know?"

"I guess I am. Yeah, I think I'm s'posed to."

"All right then. Which bus do you ride?"

"I dunno."

"Wonderful."

I was just about to ask Warner to pick his favorite colored bus, when I happened to glance down at my bus schedule. At the bottom of the page, my boss had added a special notation: *Warner Chase may ride Route 3 (Green).

"Okay, Warner, it looks like you'll be riding the Green bus home."

I heaved a sigh of relief as he boarded the bus. I watched it turn the corner, Warner's face beaming at me from the rear window. Two buses had not yet arrived, so I turned to the second page of the bus schedule. On page two, I found a notation at the bottom of the page:

*Warner Chase may ride Route 4 (Blue).

I then turned from page one to page two of my bus schedule just to make sure I wasn't imagining things. Unfortunately, the schedule did indeed contradict itself. But I didn't let this bother me for long. I was overheated and exhausted. After all, I thought, Warner is ten years old—he would have known if I had put him in the wrong bus group. Having convinced myself that everything was fine, I ran to meet my friend Dana.

Dana and I had developed a daily ritual of vegetating under the huge willow tree after work. It was a wonderful way to relieve all the tensions of the day. So, desperately anxious to relax, I ran down the huge hill to wait for my friend.

I lay back in the grass and closed my eyes. My whole body

205

relaxed as the cool breeze brushed my face. I gazed up at the hill, marveling at the picturesque landscape. The hill looked so wonderful: for once it was devoid of children running rampant. It was Dana who disturbed the perfect scene. She came bounding down the hill as if she had been shot out of a cannon. By the time she reached me, she was gasping.

"Miriam—Mrs. Chase is here! She says that Warner wasn't at the bus stop when she went to pick him up! She's waiting in Mary's office!" Terrified, I jumped to my feet. I pictured Warner lying dead in a ditch somewhere. I could not control my panic. I ranted and raved like Ophelia in *Hamlet*.

"Warner Chase may ride Route 3. Warner Chase may ride Route 4. On the other hand, Warner Chase may not ride a bus at all."

"Miriam, calm down," Dana urged. "Get hold of yourself!" (This would have been more effective had she slapped my face repeatedly while saying it.)

My boss, Mary, met us in the doorway of her office. She did not look pleased.

"Dana," she said, "Here's a list of all the kids on Route 3. Please call their parents and see if Warner went home with one of their kids."

What wonderful publicity for camp, I thought. "Hello, Mrs. Walker? We seem to have misplaced a little boy named Warner and we need to know if he happened to wander in with your Christopher?" I wondered if I was too young to collect unemployment.

I entered Mary's office to face Mrs. Chase. She was a middle-aged woman dressed like a model for *The Preppy Handbook* (there were more whales on that woman's body than in all of the Atlantic). Mrs. Chase saw me and without meeting my glance, she said, "I'm so sorry about this."

Why are you offering me your condolences? I thought wildly. It's your kid who's probably lying in a ditch somewhere.

Suddenly, I realized why Mrs. Chase was apologizing: she

knew damned well that she hadn't briefed Warner on what to do after camp. If only Mrs. Chase spent as much time thinking about Warner as she did color-coordinating her outfits. Anger welled inside me. How dare this woman make me look bad in front of my boss when she's equally to blame? Lawsuits. I'll have to sell everything I own, I thought, as I totaled my assets in my head.

Meanwhile, Mrs. Chase sat in Mary's swivel chair, her eyes still avoiding mine. She sniffled twice, then searched through her canvas whale-ridden handbag for a tissue (God forbid she should smear her makeup). Mary took over at this point and tried to console her.

"Mrs. Chase, everything will be just fine. We won't know anything until the bus service returns our call."

"It's all my fault," wailed Mrs. Chase.

You got that right, I thought.

"Noooo, Mrs. Chase. The camp is equally to blame. Please calm down. There probably isn't anything to be alarmed about."

BBBRRRIINNGGG! The phone rang. We all stared at it. Then we all stared at one another, frozen, unable to answer it. I couldn't stand the agony. I reached for the phone and without a word, handed it to Mary, who stood there, saying "Uh-huh" into the phone. Finally, she smiled, offered the phone to Mrs. Chase, and said, "Would you like to speak to your son?"

Mrs. Chase grabbed the phone. "Oh, Warner, are you all right? I've been worried sick! I guess I'll pick you up now. Or you could take a cab. Goodbye. I'll see you soon!"

"Are you going to pick Warner up now?" I asked.

"Maybe. He may be taking a cab here. Would you be willing to stay here in case he shows up?"

"You did it again! I can't believe you actually did it again! I'm getting out of here." I left. I left for good. And for all I know, Warner Chase is still riding around in a taxi somewhere, smiling out the back window with a finger up his nostril.

ESSAYS

There Are No Small Parts

I CRANED MY NECK to get a look at the *Annie Get Your Gun* cast list. My eyes scanned the rows of names. And scanned and scanned. Finally I found my name—in the lower left-hand corner of the legal-sized page, under the heading "The Chorus."

Dazed and deflated, I slowly backed away from the list, relying on the blue cinder-block wall opposite for support. I was thinking, How could this happen? After four years of playing leads! It's humiliating! I deserve much better! But I had not been given a lead, deserving or not.

I don't know what made me do what I did next. Considering my state of mind, I should have done myself and the rest of the cast a favor and gone home. Instead, I blinked back my tears and walked to the rehearsal room as if to my own execution. As I reached the wooden double doors, the thought of entering this room, to which I had always eagerly rushed, filled me with dread. Ignoring the nagging feeling in my stomach, I swung the doors open and entered.

The read-through was already in progress. Most of the cast members were perched on steps descending into the room and I spotted my friend Stephanie, a petite girl with an almost childlike figure. She had dark brown shoulder-length hair and an impish face. I sat down next to her and we shared her script. My anger was rising with each badly read line. I muttered, "This stinks. I hate this. I can't believe I'm only in the chorus. This stinks. I hate it!" I knew that my lamentations were of no use, but I continued anyway. Stephanie waited patiently for me to stop, barely acknowledging my whimperings. I went on, unable to prevent my thoughts from taking control of my mouth. Finally, Stephanie could no longer contain her anger. She turned to me, her deep brown eyes becoming slits, and hissed, "If you hate it so much, why don't you just quit?"

"Maybe I will," I replied, bristling at the harshness of her challenge. All communication between us ceased for the rest of the rehearsal. After an eternity, the rehearsal ended and I raced to catch the activity bus. Stephanie, who rode the same bus, followed me outside to the front of the school. I plopped myself down on a cement bench. Stephanie did the same on another. I stared at the ground dejectedly. When the neon yellow school bus pulled up, Stephanie walked past me without a word. I could tell by her jutting jaw that she felt contempt for me. Then, right before the bus pulled away, she stood up, leaned over and spoke directly to me.

"Miriam, you are soooo stuck up! I can't believe you! I've been in the chorus all of my life and there's nothing wrong with it. It's just as hard as being a lead—maybe even harder. How do you think all of your bitching makes me feel? If you don't like it, just get the hell out!"

She stormed to the back of the bus and I dissolved in tears. I couldn't believe Stephanie had treated me that way and yet I realized that she was doing me a favor. I had been heading for a fall that was long overdue. Stephanie was absolutely right and I hated her for it.

By the next morning, Stephanie and I had already apologized to each other and I thanked her for telling me what no one else would. I asked her to please repeat her performance if the occasion ever arose. We both giggled and I felt like a part of the human race once more.

As I walked down a crowded hallway toward my first class, another theater friend named Debbie approached me (actually, she charged me like a bull). "Did you hear the news?" she asked, bubbling over with excitement. Without waiting for my reply, she continued. "The girl who's playing Dolly quit! You'd better see Tom! You might have the part."

I ran to the rehearsal hall. When I got there, I tried my best to appear casual in front of Tom, the director. "So, Tom, what are you going to do now that Cathy has quit?" I blurted out (so much for subtlety). Tom said that he hadn't decided yet.

As I turned to go, he asked, "Wolfe, do you have a script?" I explained that I didn't, because he had said that chorus members wouldn't be needing one. "Well, let me get you one," he said, walking swiftly to his desk. Not understanding, I asked, "Why?" He turned to me and said, "I'd like you to play Dolly. Think about it, okay?"

I went home and debated for hours. I thought of what a good experience being in the chorus would be. But, hell, I took the part. How stupid do you think I am?

Sloth Log

"IF A HIPPO COULD DANCE ballet? How bizarre!" I muttered to myself as I left the dance classroom. We'd been given an assignment to study the animals at the zoo. But the more I thought about the assignment, the more sense it made to me. As an animal lover, I was thrilled to have an excuse to visit the zoo every weekend and perhaps simultaneously become less aware of missing my own pets. So, on September 7th, Pete, Mike, Tom and I set out for a Sunday at the zoo.

Pete and Mike quickly abandoned Tom and me, probably because we moved so slowly from one cage to another, commenting on everything we saw. Tom and I were fascinated by the overwhelming behavioral similarities between the animals and the people. The Japanese macaques, for example, proved particularly interesting, as they LOVE to stand close to the glass and stare intently at the zoo-goers. This struck me as very ironic, like something out of Orwell's *Animal Farm.*

In any event, somewhere between the birds and the bats, I happened upon a cage full of sloths. Tom became engrossed watching a nearby cage full of mouse lemurs; they looked like anorexic gerbils to me. The sloths moved so slowly and gracefully upside-down that I quickly got hooked on watching them. (What a strange choice of words; sloths have hooks on their hands and feet for hanging upside-down.) Oddly, sloths spend practically their entire lives upside-down: eating, sleeping and giving birth!! Sloths look like something out of *Star Wars*. Their hair is partially white and very long (as if they were cousins to Chewbaca). The sign next to the cage said sloths move so slowly that algae collects on their fur. After reading this, I understood perfectly the definition of sloth as meaning "disinclination to action or labor."

I made a note of the sloths' hunched torsos and rounded shoulders. Their long arms are jointed at the elbows and wrists. When they're not hanging upside-down, they're curled up in a ball on branches. Their noses twitching were the only quick movements I could see. I left the zoo excited, praying that I'd be allowed to use the barre for my sloth dance.

9/14. Tom grumbled incessantly as we stood on the mile-long line to enter the zoo. I was in better spirits, probably because I was anxious to see my sloths. Tom was less enthused about his mouse lemurs—after all, how psyched can you get about a little rodent??? I looked at Tom and, knowing that he was unenthused, asked, "Wouldn't it be great if we could Sloth together?" This began our month-long preoccupation with sloths.

When I first arrived on the 14th, the sloths were very active, but soon after, they stopped moving completely. The strange thing about them is that when one sloth moves, they all move—they have a sort of chain reaction to things. I discovered an actual movement of sloths that isn't slow: their scratching. When they scratch, they pluck themselves, as if they are playing the violin. I also noticed that sloths cross over their arms when they walk on the ceiling. The two baby sloths are sooo precious; they are truly valued by the older sloths. Never have I seen animals as caring as these adult sloths are to the babies. In fact, at one point, a baby sloth was being cradled in another's arms so tightly that if I hadn't seen them move into this position, I never would have known that there were two sloths in front of me!

I still couldn't get over the zoo-goers' resemblance to the animals. I couldn't believe some of the things I was hearing, so I wrote them down. Here's a small sampling of sloth-related comments:

"They have to be stuffed—they aren't moving."

"Awww-they're sooo cute!"

"EEWWWW, gross!"

"They look like Ewoks!"

And, my personal favorite: "Hey—that looks just like some people I met at a party Friday night!"

9/21. Something really funny happened. The sloths share their cage with an armadillo-like animal called the paca. The sign next to the cage says both "Sloth" and "Paca." So, a man and his wife and kids asked the question, "What are they?" The father replied, "They're pacas." Naturally, I felt compelled to set them straight. After all, the sloths deserved the best possible treatment. So I turned to the ignorant man, my eyes like slits, and hissed, "They're sloths." The man just looked at me strangely and walked away, dragging his children with him. Maybe I was spending a little too much time at the zoo!

10/5. My last zoo trip. I noticed something really interesting: sloths are always falling asleep—it doesn't matter what position they are in. And, since they're always close together, they're always waking each other up. Their little piggish faces look sooo human as they nudge each other! I've just begun to see their different personalities. The bigger ones seem to be in control of the others. For example, if a large sloth wants to go somewhere and a smaller one is in the way, the smaller sloth gets stepped on!! There are two large sloths in this cage.

Well, that pretty much raps up my log.

I really enjoyed this assignment because I learned a lot: not just Sloth Information, but a lot about myself. I've decided that zoos are not good places for me—they depress me too much. As far as I'm concerned, the Burnett Zoo's cages are much too small. But that's neither here nor there.

Now, back to the classroom to dream up my sloth dance. Thank you for giving me this unique opportunity to be creative. It truly is appreciated.

If Hogarth Had Been a Playwright

THE SIX-PAINTING SERIES entitled *Marriage à la Mode* exemplifies William Hogarth's constant struggle to expose the social ills of his day. His portrayal of eighteenth century English life is both whimsical and frighteningly accurate and reveals the hypocrisy involved in an aristocratic couple's loveless relationship. It was somewhat unusual for Hogarth to deal with an aristocratic social level. Rather, he often utilized his medium to act as a champion of the poor and the homeless, refusing to complacently accept their exploitation. *Marriage à la Mode* clearly conveys Hogarth's loathing for the vanity, greed and pretentiousness he saw cultivated by the aristocracy.

Hogarth's series could easily be transformed into an exciting theatrical event. Through his use of ironic humor, Hogarth hoped to force his audience to recognize the corruptive nature of the aristocracy's motives for marriage. Because the theater is an art form particularly well-suited to challenging the status quo, this ironic humor could provide a powerful dramatic device which perhaps would persuade the audience to recognize the hypocritical nature of his characters. It is only through that acknowledgment that change is possible. Thus, a primary purpose of Hogarth's art is consistent with that of the theater: to initiate change. So it is essential to examine the specific techniques utilized by Hogarth in order to understand why the *Marriage à la Mode* series contains such extraordinary dramatic potential.

Shortly After the Marriage, the second painting in the series, would be an ideal scene to act because Hogarth provides his viewers with an overwhelming amount of useful information about the characters. The information offered is precisely the kind necessary to the actor approaching character work.

One of the most difficult tasks an actor faces is to make the character's subtext, or inner monologue, clear. Expressing subtext proves difficult because human beings make a conscious effort to conceal their true feelings by controlling their faces, voices and physical behavior. This is not to say that Hogarth's characters are completely honest. On the contrary, they are all deceptive.

For example, any viewer of *Shortly After the Marriage* can immediately see that although the steward wants to appear pious and superior, he is obviously as hypocritical as the couple he serves. Hogarth conveys that by grossly exaggerating the steward's gesture of throwing up his hands in disgust. This gesture, combined with the steward's humorous and practiced facial expression, makes his insincerity glaringly obvious. In this case, Hogarth's genius is evident because he successfully illustrates the discrepancy between what the character would have others believe and what the character actually does. Hogarth uses body language and facial expressions to facilitate a deeper understanding of his work. The insights that Hogarth makes available would prove tremendously helpful to actors bringing the characters to life.

Hogarth's characterization of the Viscount also reveals his genius as an artist: the Viscount's body and face telegraph his feelings. The Viscount, sitting slouched in his chair, clearly suffers from exhaustion. His expression shows that he has just returned home from an evening of questionable activities! His dialogue, if this series were a play, could include these lines to express his feelings in *Shortly After the Marriage*:

"Oh, what a night I've had. (Sarcastically) And I'm so very glad to be home." Hogarth successfully reveals the Viscount's misery in every possible way.

Ronald Paulson, author of *Representations of Revolution*, accurately defines Hogarth's characterization of the Viscountess:

". . . he consistently emphasizes the connotations of disobedience, rebellion and entanglement as well as beauty."

Indeed, the entire composition suggests that the chaotic, neglected household is a direct result of the Viscountess' "rebellion" and "disobedience." The Viscount's countenance makes him look more victimized than guilty or responsible. Hogarth's agitated composition exudes chaos. His design is dominated by a combination of horizontals, verticals and fluid curves. The entire design frames the Viscountess—she is clearly meant to be the focus of the painting. In fact, this painting particularly shows that Hogarth places much of the blame on the Viscountess for the disasters that befall the couple. All the horizontal lines are drawn to the Viscountess, the central figure of the painting. The only fluid curve in the painting appears over the Viscountess, in the form of an arch. This arch frames her, again suggesting that she is primarily responsible for the already unstable marriage. Closer examination of the Viscountess' face in *Shortly After the Marriage* shows the "rebelliousness" and "disobedience" mentioned by Paulson. Her expression is one of coy smugness, as if to say to her husband, "I know what you've been up to and I couldn't care less. This is simply a marriage of convenience for me."

The fact that such dialogue is so easily written illustrates Hogarth's ability to create believable characters—characters worthy of a life on the stage. The Viscountess dominates the painting as she would dominate the stage if *Shortly After the Marriage* were a scene from a play.

The amount of detail that Hogarth puts forth is astounding, because the medium is oil. The depth of the space effectively reveals the material wealth that motivated the couple to wed in the first place. The symmetrical nature of the figures has a whimsical effect: this household is far from being stable or balanced. Hogarth adds to this irony through the use of clever details to clue the viewer in to the deception occurring.

For example, a picture hangs above the mantle, between the couple. Its subject is a cupid, complete with wings and a musical instrument. This cupid, which appears to be watching over the couple, represents everything the couple's relationship lacks: love, sincerity and pure motives. So, rather than serving as a symbol or good omen for the couple, the cupid symbolizes, instead, the nature of the deception to which the couple is party.

Perhaps the most subtle use of detail, however, reveals itself as a symbol frequently used in Hogarth's work: the dog that yaps about the Viscount's feet. According to Ronald Paulson: "[The dog is] the figure of disorder. [He] is an emphatic male principle, often a surrogate for a young woman's absent lover."

Perhaps, then, Hogarth's use of the dog is another foreshadowing technique to suggest the Viscountess' sordid affair with her attorney, Silvertongue. In any event, these details presented by Hogarth all contribute to a deep understanding of the intricacies of the characters' lives.

In *Shortly After the Marriage*, Hogarth make his viewers voyeurs of sorts. This work represents a single second in time, as if Hogarth had painted a single motion picture frame.

In most types of drama, the actor struggles to develop this sense of a "fourth wall" on stage, so that he shows no awareness of the audience. Rather, like Hogarth's viewers, the audience members act as voyeurs, peeking in on a very private reality. To stress the most important things about a potentially overwhelmingly chaotic painting, Hogarth uses a muted color scheme and nondescript lighting. The color scheme, which is a combination of earth and cooler tones, is utilized only insofar as to set a dim, oppressive atmosphere—an atmosphere devoid of hope. Similarly, it is not light itself that dominates the work; it is a lack of light. What existing light is left emanates from the sickeningly pink dress worn by the Viscountess, who, according to Hogarth, is to blame for the situation.

Hogarth's exceptional capacity to create a world within his paintings explains their extraordinary dramatic potential. As a drama, the *Marriage à la Mode* series could serve as a wonderful history lesson and, simultaneously, as a humorous, engrossing piece of entertainment.

Shortly After the Marriage alone illustrates the extraordinary nature of Hogarth's work. Its attention to detail and technical virtuosity serve as an inspiration to an infinite number of artists, this writer included!

Berthe Morisot: Underrated Artist of Our Time

THE CAPACITY FOR PERCEIVING the poetry inherent in the everyday world, and of communicating it to others, is the gift of only a few beings—persons with a special grace that makes them authentic artists or poets.

Berthe Morisot had that unique capacity as one of only three women to be actively involved in the Impressionist movement from its inception. Although considered exceptional by her contemporaries, her work was often dismissed by historians as inferior to that of her male contemporaries, or accused of possessing particularly "feminine" qualities. This attempt to de-emphasize Morisot's genius is a prime example of the subtle sexism which has pervaded and continues to pervade our culture.

Our contemporary female playwrights share the difficulty of being artists in the midst of a male-dominated movement. Despite the fact that more and more women are gaining recognition in the theater for holding top positions, extraordinary female playwrights are difficult to find. The reasons for this lie in the fact that those with exceptional ability constantly are undermined by threatened men.

In l860, when Berthe was nineteen and her sister Edma was twenty, the two became students of a naturalistic artist, Camille Corot, whose work had a profound influence on all the Impressionists. Berthe and Edma were sent to Corot by their former teacher, the historical painter Guichard. From him, the girls had learned the fundamentals of painting: the value of light, shadow and color. Guichard reluctantly yielded his teaching to Corot upon his realization that Berthe was bound and determined to paint outdoors.

Corot's style has been called a "lyrical, misty painting technique." The soft, unusual light of the area around Paris called the Ile-de-France inspired him the most. He passed this source of inspiration on to the Morisot sisters. Corot is credited with having helped Berthe develop an element of her work which distinguishes her: her use of early morning light. She is said to have "conveyed on her canvases the pale gold of the dawn."

Aimé Millet, wife of painter Jean Millet, wrote Berthe and her sister: "You are reproached for painting like Corot. In the first place, it is not true . . . and further, I regard this kind of reproach as praise."

In his biography *Berthe Morisot*, Jean Dominique Rey writes: "If we had to define Berthe Morisot's originality we might describe her as a painter of the early morning light. And for that Corot is responsible." Rey's comment contains a subtle but stinging message; it implies that she blindly copied Corot. Dispelling this misconception is critical to an in-depth study of her work.

Corot undoubtedly had a substantial influence on her. However, he felt that Berthe took far too many liberties in her work, which made her, in his eyes, less disciplined. He preferred her sister as a student. Ironically, Corot was wary of exactly the element in Berthe's work that gained her notoriety and, later, acceptance by the Impressionists. Corot, although progressive, was not a member of the Impressionist movement. Berthe's work possessed his misty, light-filled quality. However, she possessed her own unique sense of natural light and its effects on objects touched by it.

An early work, *Thatched Cottage in Normandy*, is a wonderful example of her individual strengths. Morisot's distinctive colors and brushstrokes are evident. The glints of white in the grass, applied with fresh, wild, dry strokes, give *Thatched Cottage* a sense of movement and of slight disturbance of the calm in the picture. These glints of white show a distinct understanding of light and its effect on nature. The only direct evidence of Corot's influence is the fact that this is a pure landscape. Morisot did few landscapes without people in them.

An overwhelming number of critics in the visual and performing arts have been and continue to be male. Unfortunately, this domination allows these men to inflict their anti-women values on the public.

Rey gives Corot the credit for Morisot's gifts. He does so, perhaps subconsciously, out of the belief that women are not capable of exceptional work of this kind. Much the same is the attitude today toward women playwrights. If a female playwright writes from her own point of view, she is considered to be writing from outside our culture. Male-dominated values are considered the universal values. Women who write from an authentic point of view risk that their subjects will be dismissed as secondary. Morisot managed, while only in her twenties, to create works like *Thatched Cottage*, defying the idea that women artists cannot create art that has universal appeal.

In the 1870s, her work was referred to as "charming," "feminine" and "delicate." In truth, the qualities that defined her work were shared with two male contemporaries: Monet and Renoir. All three artists devoted themselves to creating a feeling of spontaneity in their work through the use of wild, free, broad brushstrokes and a pastel-oriented palette.

Morisot was restricted by her gender. For example, she sat for many portraits by her good friend and mentor, Edouard Manet. However, she herself could not ask her male contemporaries to sit for her: it was considered improper because of her unmarried status. As a woman, Morisot was not permitted to join the painters who met in the Paris cafes. From their cafe lives, the male Impressionists gleaned a great deal of material forbidden to her. So, despite the obstacle of being limited to painting landscapes, mother/ child (and later husband/child) scenes and still lifes, Morisot still proved influential in the Impressionist movement.

Her *Summer's Day*, which was shown at the Impressionist Exhibition of l880, broke new ground, preceding Monet's painting of the same subject by ten years. In this open air scene and others like it, white paint proves an essential element for Morisot. Faces are almost consumed by the sunlight hitting them—they receive no detail. This element shows the effect of watercolors, at which Morisot was very skilled, on her oil paintings. The picture produces the sensation of a single moment in time, a moment in which the subjects are completely at one with their surroundings. This painting's impression is that of lightness and spontaneity.

Comparing Morisot's *Summer's Day* with Renoir's *The Seine at Asnières*, both painted in l879, dispels many misconceptions. It is obvious that the critics' preoccupation with her work's "feminine" quality resulted (and still results) from their own inability to see her as a skilled artist, whose work rivaled that of her male contemporaries. Even more ironically, Renoir's painting is void of the "masculine toughness" that men's paintings possess, according to past and present critics. Renoir's *Seine at Asnières* uses a very similar palette and brushstrokes no less fluttery, "delicate," or "feminine" than Morisot's. In my humble opinion, Renoir's *Seine* lacks the extraordinary freedom achieved by Morisot in *Summer's Day*. This can be attributed to her unique use of white, thick paint to achieve the feeling of morning light. For this wonderful quality, she alone is responsible.

After Morisot's death in l895, a huge retrospective exhibition was launched at the Musée de Luxembourg. At that time, many people argued that Impressionism involved the recording of surface appearances only. Even more infuriating, this narrow-minded and ignorant claim was used as a reason to explain the presence of women in the Impressionist movement. Women were believed to have a nature "more facile and fluent than men's," according to art critic George Moore. "[They] do things more easily than men, but do not penetrate below the surface." Thus, Impressionism was deemed a "feminine" movement because of its superficiality and simplistic theology.

This idea is both outrageous and false. Morisot's perspective was neither superficial nor simplistic. On the contrary, she had extraordinary insight, largely due to the self-doubts which plagued her throughout her life. Morisot's art tortured her—it proved to be her greatest sadness as well as her greatest joy. Her life, despite her successes, was permeated by persistent feelings of sadness and discouragement. She drove herself relentlessly; her expectations were uncompromisingly high.

Berthe's sister, Edma, gave up painting for marriage, not without some regret. This subject of family versus a career caused great inner turmoil in Morisot's life. It prompted her to paint a picture which reveals her depth as a painter and a human being. For this reason, *The Cradle* is probably her greatest achievement. *The Cradle* shows Edma (Madame Pontillon) seated and staring into the cradle, which contains her newborn infant. The mother's expression is contemplative and melancholy, rather than blindly content. This picture shows a woman who has sacrificed her life's work, her art, to have a family. *The Cradle* accurately reveals the emotional turmoil that accompanies this decision.

Morisot later married Eugene Manet (Edouard's brother) and had a daughter, Julie. They provided her with an infinite number of subjects for her painting. She successfully balanced her work and her family.

Most women in the 1980s still struggle hard to achieve this—many without success. Gretchen Cryer, author of the books for musicals such as *Hanging Onto the Good Times* and *I'm Getting My Act Together and Taking It on the Road*, expressed this not-so-modern dilemma:

"The writer who has children is usually primarily consumed with being a mother. She is able to pursue a writing career at home if someone else—a husband, for example—is supporting the family. But if she is struggling for money, a woman can hardly justify sitting at home writing a play, if family survival dictates a second income. . . [You] find that your experience has definitely deepened from having children . . .The negative part is—compared to a man's life, you've been at home. Therefore, you're probably going to write about cloistered subjects . . . and then get criticized for writing kitchen drama."

Today many male critics still negate the validity of a plot only on the basis of their own narrow experience. Usually, the plays attacked include male characters portrayed with unflattering personality flaws and characteristics. "I don't believe she'd stay with him," or "I don't believe she wouldn't see a psychiatrist." Critics pretend to be "arbiters of human behavior." Since they themselves wouldn't behave in a particular way, the basic premise is wrong.

Critics also frequently accuse female playwrights of writing "brutal" male characters. This is a simplistic attitude on the part of the critics: a playwright must believe in and love all her characters. Simply because a male character doesn't represent a heroic figure does not mean necessarily that he represents evil incarnate either. Many male critics automatically judge the works of female playwrights with this ridiculous criterion. It seems that the critics, rather than the playwrights, reveal themselves simplistic in their views.

The longstanding sexist practices which have pervaded our culture since much before Morisot's time robbed her of the recognition she deserved. She contributed substantially to the Impressionist movement and inspired many other artists. In order to prevent female artists of the future from being robbed of credit that is their due, women must challenge the institutions that perpetuate sexism.

The recent book *Interviews with Contemporary Women Playwrights* claims that women playwrights are daring to challenge the "universal" and redefining culture. In doing so, they are broadening our sense of the range of human possibility.

ACCORDING to the editor of *Women's Art Journal*, Berthe Morisot has now been accepted as a major contributor to Impressionism. Miriam would be delighted to know that. (Hey, maybe she does.)

POEMS

In the Crevices of My Mind

Hands pushing my chest scrambling to
  reach my neck,
Hands that trample,
Hands that scrape,
Hands that grope for self-justification in the crevices
  of my soul.
They slap. They sting.
I want to cut them up.
  How dare you! I want to scream.
  They are indignant without cause.

But I don't. I swallow and my heart jumps up to meet
  my throat. I've shrunk four inches.
Queasy with cowardice, my hands tremble, and I circle
  my cardboard box.
Once, twice, three times I circle round.
 My cheeks continue to burn
  long after my last lap is complete.

DURING HER summer job at Darien Lake State Park in upstate
New York, she lived with a family of five, including their fourteen-
month-old baby. Her summer mom sent me a copy of a long letter
Miriam wrote her from London. Here's the last paragraph:

Dear Darlene: . . . .I really miss hearing pounding on my door
followed by "Mimi, Mimi, Mimi, Mimi!" every morning.
(You never thought I'd say that, did you?) Enclosed is a poem
I wrote this summer. It really sums up my feelings about your
house as my home and the sense of peace I felt there. Please
think of it as a giant hug from me to you. Darlene, I miss
you terribly and am anxious to hear how you're doing. Please
take good care of yourself and stay in touch! Love, Miriam.

A Summer Evening in Corfu, New York

A lavender sky
    and I, etched in black against it
    as I hang my damp
       summer
           garments
   upon the line.

The sky and the meadow
    sense me here as I perform this ritual
hanging my clothes
    one
       by
          one
on the line.

A mist hangs, filling the space
F I L L I N G   T H E   S P A C E
    about the frayed grasses
       beyond the garden.
And the purple clover flowers
    wait motionless
    for the mist to engulf them.

I am here with the meadow
making my silent pact
    with the summer sky
as I
    hang my clothes
    (one
       by
          one)
on the line.
    to dry.

225

IN HER small Paris journal, she wrote this:

> 10/2/88. Manet's painting *Olympia*—a prostitute. The prostitute's subtext: "You want it, you'll have to pay for it." Prostitutes were the first women of power. They were the only financially independent women: women were either wives/mothers or prostitutes. Manet was pointing out the hypocrisy of men who went to prostitutes. We're voyeurs in the picture.

The Prostitute

She holds her head high
and angled; her chin and
    her whole being reek defiance.
She does not ask
Do you want me?
She says, plainly, You can have me—for a price.
And you do want me, my darling.
I am your angel—wrap me in a white sheath.
I'll wrap you up.
I don't need you,
You need me—all of me.
Come here. Trust.
It's just a little joke, darling.
No need to get upset.
We'll just stay here for awhile—don't waste time
    with regrets.
I never do.
Regret nothing. Forgive everything.
God knows, I do.

WHEN MIRIAM went off to college, I discovered an issue of *Soap Opera Stars* in the top drawer of her dresser. It was stuffed full of *General Hospital* photos that she had saved since she was thirteen. In junior high, she wrote this poem about her favorite *GH* character, Anne Logan, played by Susan Pratt (1982). Miriam sent her a pair of purple socks, supposedly the actress's favorite color. Ms. Pratt never replied. (Maybe she never even received them.) After Miriam died, I published her poem with an introduction in *Soap Opera Stars,* August 1993.

Annie's Song

I can't say I'm too happy
About the new Annie.
She's got me deeply worried,
I mean, she's really hurried
Into trouble with one Doctor Noah Drake.
Her friends tried with all their might
To make Annie see the light.
But Annie doesn't really care
If everyone is in despair.
Meanwhile, Bobbie's turning green,
Too much of Anne, Noah's seen,
So Anne please be the way you were.
You must believe me, I am sure
That you were better off that way.
Oh—and Annie—start today!

A Conversation with Grandpa Saul

MY FATHER, Dr. Saul K. Pollack, visited us twice a year from his home in Milwaukee. The year Miriam was nine Grandpa Saul brought with him a tiny pocket tape recorder. He recorded two conversations he and Miriam had over the weekend—one in our living room and the next one on a walk they took together. He saved the tape, and after he died in 1991, my brother, John Pollack, discovered it in a drawer in Father's desk.

It was a Sunday morning and Miriam played a short piano piece for him. She was also just learning the clarinet and played a squeaky version of "Mary Had a Little Lamb."

Grandpa:	Beautiful! Beautiful! Come and sit with me and tell me what you were doing in Sunday School this morning.
Miriam:	Learning Hebrew and poems and stuff and we were studying about Judah, who led the Israelites, Cain and all that stuff.
Grandpa:	I am very impressed with that new vocabulary you have. All these enormous words you use.
Miriam:	You can feel my feet and see how cold they are.
Grandpa:	Oh really? Oh, you are freezing! How many kids were in your group that you came home with now from Sunday School?
Miriam:	Ummm. Six, including me.
Grandpa:	Who were they?
Miriam:	Well, they were all boys and I am the only girl.
Grandpa:	Oh, really? Do you like that?
Miriam:	No.

Grandpa:	How come?
Miriam:	I don't.
Grandpa:	Why not?
Miriam:	Because they are all stupid. [She laughs.]
Grandpa:	Are they stupid?
Miriam:	No, they are not stupid, but they are not the best people in the world.
Grandpa:	Is that right? Do they tease?
Miriam:	No, it's just that I am mad at one of them. This boy, Jeff, he can be really mean sometimes. Not to me, but one time when we were walking home from school, he started a fight with one of my friends. Jeff pushed her down and she got a scratch on her brand-new glasses.
Grandpa:	Oh. You said you were going to make up some riddles. And?
Miriam:	And send them to a publisher.
Grandpa:	Yes. And then what do you hear from them?
Miriam:	Well, what do you mean?
Grandpa:	I mean, if the publisher doesn't accept the riddles, what do they send you?
Miriam:	They send you a letter saying, "Dear Contributor: We regret to inform you that your manuscript does not suit our present needs" or something like that.
Grandpa:	Do they encourage you to write some more?
Miriam:	It depends if they like it or not.

229

Grandpa: Where did you find out about that?

Miriam: In a book I was reading.

Grandpa: Oh, in a book you were reading about publishing.

Miriam: Yes.

Grandpa: Oh. Are you going to make up your own riddles?

Miriam: Yes, I have some, eight of them.

Grandpa: Really? When are you going to complete that?

Miriam: I have no idea. It depends on how fast I can get thirty riddles.

Grandpa: You need thirty?

Miriam: I asked my parents how many would be good for a book. And they said thirty.

Grandpa: They thought about thirty. That will be interesting to send to a children's book publisher.

Miriam: And if they don't like it, I will just write another!

Grandpa: Keep trying. That's the idea. You call that persevering, don't you? You know that word?

Miriam: Not exactly.

Grandpa: Well, to persevere means to keep at it until you succeed.

Miriam: Yeah.

Grandpa: And you are willing to do that, aren't you?

Miriam: Yes.

Grandpa: What are you eating there?

Miriam: A cookie. Want one?

Grandpa:	Sure.
Miriam:	See that white house across the street? The person that lives there, he is in second grade. He's a brat.
Grandpa:	He's a brat?
Miriam:	Yes. And down the street you know Shannon. And there's Shannon's best friend, who is Kimberly.
Grandpa:	Yes.
Miriam:	I am Shannon's second best friend.
Grandpa:	Oh, are you? Well, who is your first best friend?
Miriam:	My first best is Tammy Noble.
Grandpa:	Oh, that's right. How often do you see Tammy?
Miriam:	Hardly often.
Grandpa:	Don't they come over?
Miriam:	No. I don't think they miss our family at all.
Grandpa:	Oh, I don't think that's true. Aren't they far away, though?
Miriam:	They aren't far away. Not in the Pasadena real far away. There's a Pasadena here, you know, next to Severna Park. They live there.
Grandpa:	Well, I would think that would be a little clumsy to come over often. I thought you were very nice friends and you did miss each other.
Miriam:	Yeah.
Grandpa:	Do they go to another school?
Miriam:	Yes, and I asked my mom. I said to my mom, "I don't think they miss us" and she said "I think

they miss us, but they do like where they live."

Grandpa:	Oh, I see. They like where they live now. Did Mr. Noble come and help fix the kitchen?
Miriam:	Yes, he did. Mr. Noble's a handyman and Mrs. Noble works as a bartender.
Grandpa:	Does she really? So they all help each other.
Miriam:	Yeah.
Grandpa:	She is a nice lady.
Miriam:	Yes. Tammy thinks she is too old for me.
Grandpa:	She is a little older, isn't she?
Miriam:	Yes, but, you know, she is only two years.
Grandpa:	I guess that does make quite a difference, she is going on eleven.
Miriam:	No it doesn't!
Grandpa:	Don't you think so?
Miriam:	No! Why don't you keep your tape recorder here at our house?
Grandpa:	Well, sometimes I like to turn it on at home and listen to you talk.
Miriam:	And you have it turned on now? Oh, Grandpa!
Grandpa:	Yeah. That's okay. Tell me more about your kitten and the winter.
Miriam:	Well, by the time it's summer, he's grown his winter coat and then he has to get rid of it because it's so hot. [She giggles.]
Grandpa:	Yeah. That's right.

232

Miriam:	And in winter, you know, now he has his light coat because he finally got rid of this winter one. Now he has to gain it back again. [She laughs.]
Grandpa:	Can other children pet him?
Miriam:	Yes. Shannon can pet him. The Nobles don't have any problem with him. So those two people—and, it depends, sometimes my other friends.
Grandpa:	In school, which is your favorite subject?
Miriam:	My favorite subject? That's a hard one. Recess! [They both laugh.]
Grandpa:	Oh, you.
Miriam:	Oh, I know my favorite subject. Dismissal!
Grandpa:	[He laughs.] But, what do you really enjoy? I hear you are quite good in math.
Miriam:	Oh, I'm OK. I like math.
Grandpa:	But which do you really excel in or enjoy the most?
Miriam:	Reading and spelling.
Grandpa:	Did you get pretty far in the spelling bee?
Miriam:	Yeah, I only missed on one word.
Grandpa:	What was it?
Miriam:	Gymnasium.
Grandpa:	Ah, can you spell it today?
Miriam:	Gymnasium. G Y M N A S I U M.
Grandpa:	That is correct. How did you miss it? How did you spell it?

Miriam:	Well, it was hard. I don't know how I spelled it.
Grandpa:	That's pretty much fun, though. You like reading, I know, because you have such beautiful books.
Miriam:	I love to read. I don't like the subject too much because I don't like the work they give you. [They're taking a walk around the block now.]
Grandpa:	On the whole, are you a pretty good sport?
Miriam:	What?
Grandpa:	Are you sporting? Can you lose without pouting?
Miriam:	Yes.
Grandpa:	That's a good thing to learn too, isn't it?
Miriam:	Yes.
Grandpa:	Sometimes you win, sometimes you lose.
Miriam:	Yes. You saw me, Grandpa. I was a good sport when we played Othello and you won.
Grandpa:	Yeah. Of course, I am such a champ at that game.
Miriam:	Oh, really? Oh, really? I even had to teach you how to play!
Grandpa:	Oh, honey, I was lucky. You know I was lucky, didn't you?
Miriam:	Yes.
Grandpa:	Because I didn't know the game. Can you play chess? I thought you learned to play chess from your father.
Miriam:	No. I'm not very good at it.
Grandpa:	Well, you will have to have him teach you because

234

he's a chess player.

Miriam: I know. He's a good one, too. Can you play chess?

Grandpa: No, I never learned it. It's a good game.

Miriam: Yes, it is a good game to play. See? Our walk led us right back home again.

Grandpa: I know, I remember, I've taken this walk with you before.

Also by Rosemary & Larry Mild

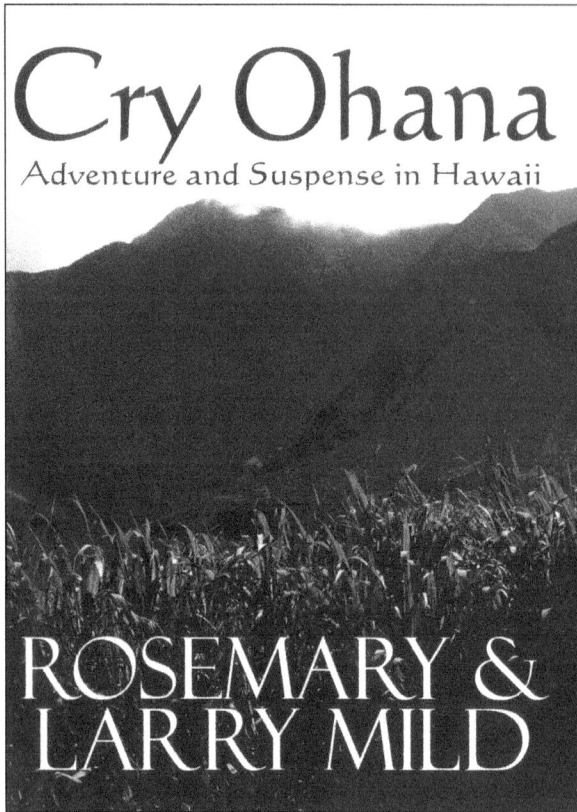

Cry Ohana
Adventure and Suspense in Hawaii

ROSEMARY &
LARRY MILD

Murder, blackmail and passion thrust a Hawaiian ohana (family) into the tentacles of Honolulu's dark side. Kekoa, the teenage son, witnesses the murder of his Uncle Big John and must flee from the killer. Danger erupts at a Filipino wedding, at a Maui resort and amid the Big Island's volcanic steam vents as the family struggles to reunite and bring down the killer.

Available on Amazon.com, Kindle and Nook.

PRAISE FOR *Cry Ohana*

"*Cry Ohana* is certainly a page-turner, and the authors seem to have a good take on the evolving concept of "ohana" and fractured families in modern Hawaii, and the action proceeds in a logical and gripping pace....The characters in this large novel are all drawn well...." **—Burl Burlingame,** *Honolulu Star Advertiser*

"*Cry Ohana* captures the essence of Hawaii while providing a suspenseful adventure about family, redemption, hope, and justice.... The use of Hawaiian slang and references to historical landmarks adds to the authenticity and flow of the story. A thrilling Hawaiian journey." **—Kathryn Franklin,** *San Francisco Book Review*

"Shame can tear families apart, and murder can obliterate them....A story of family and reunion for the betterment of it all, and dedicated to Hawaiian culture. A choice pick, highly recommended." **—Margaret Lane,** *Midwest Book Review*

"I was hooked from the very first page. There is plenty of suspense, intrigue, blackmail and betrayal. The characters are very easy to connect with. The descriptions of Hawaii are excellent. A book you won't want to miss." **—2011 Gold Seal** *Reader's Favorite* **Award**

"Rosemary and Larry Mild bring us a struggle that makes *Cry Ohana* such a compelling story....Chase scenes and plot twists abound. We are given murder and blackmail as well as human pathos and drama in abundance. *Cry Ohana* is an exciting and poignant story rating a 9 of 10 on the Weaver meter." **—Sid Weaver,** *Mainly Mysteries*

"This book was very endearing....My heart went out to Kekoa. I was able to relate to his struggle of survival....Even the patience and tenacity Leilani had, never wanting to give up on finding her family, was inspiring....I recommend this book and these authors." **—Nikkea Smithers, Pres., Romance Writers of America Book Club**

Also by Rosemary & Larry Mild

The Paco and Molly Mystery Series

Locks and Cream Cheese—set in an old Chesapeake Bay mansion full of hidden rooms, locked doors and secrets out of the past. A million dollar painting and a jeweled key are the prizes, but are murder and trickery worth it? The wily police detective and housekeeper/cook are on the case.

Hot Grudge Sunday—Paco and Molly, finding love and marriage, go on a honeymoon bus tour out West. Bank robbers, conspirators and murderers interrupt their bliss and once more they are called upon to uncover spine-chilling schemes as spectacular as Zion, the Grand Canyon and Yellowstone.

Boston Scream Pie—A young girl's persisting nightmare leads Paco and Molly to the Boston family household, where the children churn up vicious undercurrents that threaten two families. Four deceased husbands lie in Mom's past. When another family member dies under mysterious circumstances, the clues point to murder. Paco and Molly see through the sinister connections and set things right.

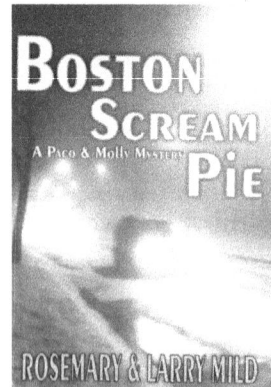

Available on Amazon.com, Kindle and Nook.

Locks and Cream Cheese

"A light-hearted book with likable characters."
—Sandra Travis-Bildah, *Washington Post*

"It's a one-of-a-kind upstairs-downstairs story, and it happens here on the Chesapeake Bay. I loved the book."
—Kathy Harig, Owner, Mystery Loves Company
Booksellers, Oxford, MD

"This caper is full of surprises, a tale with love, hate, lust and greed. The Maryland background makes a good setting for the action. A promising first novel." *—BooksnBytes*

"A Million-Dollar Painting Disappears—Curious? So were we. Especially since the painting is stolen from a museum on the shore of the Chesapeake Bay and the sleuths fall in love. Molly Mesta, a roly-poly cook, and Paco LeSoto, a retired detective, solve the museum mystery." **—Kathryn McKay,** *Washington Woman*

"How [can] any couple spend so much time together and not produce real-life mayhem? The [Milds] get along and it shows in their increasingly successful publishing ventures."
—Joni Guhne, *Baltimore Sun*

"Like retired detective Paco LeSoto and his accomplice Molly Mesta, the Milds enjoy collaborating because they've come up with a formula that works." **—Orly Rosenberg,** *Baltimore Jewish Times*

Hot Grudge Sunday

"The reader gets to share the sights and delights of the Southwest while sharing the puzzle with all its multiple parts that seem not to fit together. The finale of this mystery will surprise you. Rosemary and Larry Mild have a real knack for pulling the bad guys out of a hat without the reader knowing who is the real villain."
—F.L. Swinford, *Gumshoe Magazine*

"*Hot Grudge Sunday* takes us on a delightful action packed ride. The story is full of surprises and kept me riveted. I'm already looking forward to Molly's next adventure."

—Mary Ellen Hughes, Author of the Craft Corner Mysteries

"Working in tandem, the authors created scenic vistas, lively characters, and enough plot twists and tension to carry the reader swiftly to the finish."   **—Edie Dykeman, Amazon review**

"The Wild West is a lot wilder whenever the Milds' tour bus arrives in *Hot Grudge Sunday*. Rosemary and Larry had me hanging by my fingernails throughout the trip. They also gave me an enticing glimpse of a part of America I've never seen. A great read."

—Robin Hathaway, Agatha Award-winning
Author of the Dr. Andrew Fenimore Mystery Series

"I had not read any of Paco and Molly's adventures before *Hot Grudge Sunday*. That will be changing. I really enjoyed them and their adventurous spirit. I can't wait to read more! I highly recommend this book!"   **—Dawn Dowdle, *Mystery Lovers Corner***

Boston Scream Pie

"We have added *Boston Scream Pie* to our recommended reading list....It is worth picking up. There is a little of something down there for everyone."   **—John Raab, *Suspense Magazine***

"...In Chapter One I met a woman who I decided I hated immediately. And she was sleeping! The case twists and turns....and kept me glued to the pages until the end."

—Kaye Barley, *Meanderings and Muses*

"If you want a light and funny mystery to read, I would definitely recommend *Boston Scream Pie*."   **—*Mystery Reader***

"If you enjoy cliff-hanging, crisis-to-crisis mysteries filled with suspense, then you are going to enjoy *Boston Scream Pie*....Deftly written and highly recommended...plays fair with the reader...."

—*Mystery Bookshelf*

"....I was fascinated by a tale that had a little dab of V.C. Andrews mixed with a bit of Leeann Sweeney. But, believe it or not, the Milds pulled it off and *voilá*, it was a winner. I loved it!....This mystery sparkles 'n shines and if there is such a thing as a V.C. Andrews 'cozy' you'll love it!" **—*Feathered Quill Book Reviews***

"*Boston Scream Pie* is a page-turning novel of suspense that will hold the reader's attention from beginning to end." **—*TCM Reviews***

"*Boston Scream Pie* was heartwarming, but suspenseful. It has a surprise ending that will shock you....one of the best novels I have read in quite a long time! It shows a very familiar part of life; true things that can really happen to people, and was just so delightful!" **—Gina Holland, *Rebecca's Read***

"This mystery provides page-turning excitement without the inordinately graphic gore to make it unpalatable. Full of injuries, illnesses, and attacks, the book shares murders and mayhem in a lower key than that sung by Hannibal Lecter. This well-researched theme causes one to wonder which individuals in the story are related—or are they at all?" **—Patty Inglish, MS., *Armchair Interviews***

"The Milds have whipped up another pleasing concoction in this charming series with their likeable protagonists, clever plotting, and generous dashes of humor. Paco and Molly are astute detectives and Molly's malaprops are as tasty as her kugel. *Boston Scream Pie* is a thoroughly enjoyable treasure." **—Anne White, Author of the *Lake George Mystery Series***

"....the plot and outcome were all carefully drawn with a resolution that I am sure will satisfy most readers. I should also note that there is a bit of sexual content as well, though nothing very graphic or gratuitous—I felt that it was pertinent to the storyline. My rating: 4.5 out of 5 stars. I recommend *Boston Scream Pie*." **—Melissa, *Mystery Mondays***

A fast, charming read. **—*Futures Mystery Anthology magazine***

Photograph by Craig Herndon

ROSEMARY MILD, mother of Miriam Luby Wolfe, is an award-winning essayist and coauthor of novels and short stories with her husband, Larry. Rosemary's essays have appeared in the *Washington Post, Baltimore Sun, Washington Woman, Generations, Quiet Mountain Essays* and elsewhere. A graduate of Smith College, she also gives talks on "From Hurt to Healing: Writing Your Personal Story."

E-mail us at: roselarry@magicile.com
Visit us at: www.magicile.com

www.ingramcontent.com/pod-product-compliance
Lightning Source LLC
Chambersburg PA
CBHW072100020426
42334CB00017B/1585